HAPPINESS IS OVERRATED

-

LIVE THE
INSPIRED LIFE
INSTEAD

ELAINA NOELL

Edited by Lisa Brew-Miller

Published by Elaina Noell
elaina@happinessisoverrated.com
www.happinessisoverrated.com

Book Layout © 2015 BookDesignTemplates.com

Happiness Is Overrated – Live the Inspired Life Instead/ Elaina Noell. --
1st ed.
ISBN 978-0-9967766-0-8

SPECIAL THANKS TO:

Lisa Brew-Miller, dear friend and editor. I'll learn not to use "nor" in my next book, I promise!

Dr. Anne Tomin, therapist. Your unique talent gave me the tools and environment needed to discover my true self and experience true happiness for the first time. The universe led me to you, and you led me to the life I was always intended to enjoy, for which I am eternally grateful.

Melody Beattie, author. *Codependent No More*[1] literally changed my life overnight. Your style of sharing your insight was exactly what I needed when I needed it.

Iyanla Vanzant, life coach I've never met. I get tremendous joy from your fearless truth seeking and bold approach underwritten with love.

Ronda Giangreco, Pam Chanter, Jessica, Louis Edlinger, Brigitte Thériault, Xerxes Whitney, Lorenzo Dughi, interviewees. Your time and kindness offered to be part of this project means so much. I had many unreturned interview requests, and what I gained from speaking with you spans far greater than pages could ever capture.

Those that have supported and inspired me with devoted love, support and friendship throughout this unpredictable journey of life.

Tanner Hirakida, who supported me throughout the creation of this book with unwavering love and encouragement.

CONTENTS

Preface

Many people react in a funny way to the title of this book. How can happiness be overrated? What can be challenged about happiness? Why do I have to live the inspired life *instead*?

There has been much discussion and research on happiness, trying to understand how to truly experience it, but what if we've had it all wrong with our "pursuit of happiness" tunnel vision?

While we know happiness is important, meaningful and impactful, we don't always understand it. We know when we feel it, but not always how to get there. Much of our happiness is circumstantial or temporary, instead of originating from a foundation of core, unwavering, *pure* happiness.

On my own elusive path of pursuing happiness, I discovered a new way to view this quest. By replacing the pursuit of happiness with seeking inspiration, we create immediate, actionable and meaningful experiences that fast track us to connecting with our true selves, and therefore to experience the pure, lasting happiness we all desire and deserve.

My exploration of the role of inspiration in my life began when my then-husband and I started building ub:inspired. Beginning as an idea for an app, the company soon showed many other opportunities, all around the concept of how inspiration can lead to your happiest and healthiest life. As I began to explore the concept of inspiration, wanting to "test" how our app could be used by "real people," I realized I needed to be one of those "real people" who live the inspired life.

Looking for inspiration, I started waking up at 5:15am to watch the sunrise a few times a week. It was dark and cold, but magical when the light started to change and the wildlife began to join the scene.

Getting up extra early, before a day of work, did not make me happy. But it sure made me feel inspired. That's when I first realized that there's a difference between feeling happy and feeling inspired.

Running is another perfect example of something that actually made me quite miserable. Happiness had absolutely nothing to do with my struggle and determination to run. It was inspiration that fueled my effort, and it was a real effort for me!

As I focused on seeking inspiration, inspiration also began finding me. The law of attraction kicked in. Allowing myself to indulge in these moments of inspiration helped me to discover and create more moments to feel inspired. And it felt amazing.

I was struggling to be happy in the way I thought I wanted to be. I knew I needed a change, but I didn't know what it was. Everything in this book is a proven testament of how I changed and improved my experience of life through experiencing more inspiration and through understanding and breaking through ceilings of happiness.

The irony of this book's title is that, in the end, we all do want to be happy. But we want to be truly happy, exuding happiness from the core of our true selves. We want happiness to be our foundation and not the overrated surface happiness for which we often settle.

The title is also intended to specifically address that putting happiness on a pedestal and worrying so much about our path towards it is futile. Instead, I'll share a new perspective that provides instant access to what we enjoy about happiness; one that is so natural and enjoyable, you won't even be thinking about it. You won't be strategizing and wondering if these steps are the key to the "destination" we call happiness because you'll be fulfilled through inspiration.

You can cheat the path to true happiness by leaving it alone—by leaving the happiness we've come to know, expect and accept out of the equation. I've found an actionable mindset more meaningful and authentic than "fake it 'til you make it." It's cheaper and faster than years of therapy (that I completely condone, for the record. I just won't be addressing that process in this book). It doesn't require medication, money or an excess of time. It's the easiest way to discover and connect with your true self. You can apply it to every aspect of life, and it's the solution for those of us who think we're too busy, too stuck or not good enough to change our lives for the better.

Inspiration dissolves excuses, removes codependency (in this case, wanting to and acting on making others happy more than making ourselves happy); and it is the quickest tool to connecting with our true selves to build and enjoy the truly happy and inspired life we all want to live.

This book is not meant to address a comprehensive solution to physical chemical imbalances, trauma recovery or addiction. There are many available resources better suited to help in those areas. I am in no way undervaluing or being frivolous about the seriousness of those conditions and what they may require for healing. I do, however, believe that this book can make a difference in the quality of life of anyone, regardless of personal circumstances.

This book is meant to be accessible, unobtrusive and encouraging, providing a new opportunity to re-frame what we think about happiness and to expand the amount of opportunities we have to enjoy life. This book doesn't expect you to be perfect, to take each line and apply it immediately or forever. It's okay to take a lot or a little from these pages. This book is your friend and partner to finding an easier way to experience and enjoy life—by living the inspired life.

"We discover the vast difference between living and feeling alive when we discover inspiration."

—Elaina Noell

STEP 1:

Stop Settling for the Happiness We've Come to Know, Expect and Accept

"If you want to change something,
you have to change something."

—Unknown

CHAPTER ONE

The Overrated Happiness We've Come to Know, Expect and Accept

As humans, we desperately want to be happy. We *need* to be happy. We pursue happiness, chase happiness, and force happiness. We worry about our happiness, we put happiness on a pedestal, we make happiness dependent on events that may occur in the future, and we hold ourselves hostage from happiness until we reach a goal. We know we want happiness, but the path to it is elusive, and the preservation of it is a promise that often can't be fulfilled. There are unhappy side effects of the happiness we've come to know, expect and accept. The system is flawed.

Let's redefine what we're really after—that feeling of unshakable fulfillment, joy, being present and being connected to our truest selves. The quickest way to get here is not by ambling and obsessing about the limited pursuit of happiness, but by the immediate and actionable pursuit to be inspired.

DEFINING HAPPINESS

This book is not intended for the fortunate few who have already mastered true happiness, rooted in their true selves and creating an unshakable foundation of happiness that starts from within. This book is intended for the rest of us who have come to know, expect and accept less than that true unshakable happiness in exchange for what feels more like accessible bouts of temporary happiness. This kind of happiness is better than nothing, but when did "nothing" become our acceptable standard? In the following scenario, let's explore the differences between the path to the happiness we've come to know, expect and accept and the path to the true happiness we desire and deserve.

Metaphorically close your eyes and imagine a hill. Picture a home on top, and imagine yourself inside the front room of this home, looking at your front door. You see an old-fashioned keyhole, big enough to look through. You approach the keyhole and discover a magical land of delight on the other side. In this world is everything you love doing, seeing and experiencing. You can see all of your favorite hobbies and activities. You see arenas and theaters filled with your favorite sports teams, musicians, and plays. You can see your favorite vistas from your favorite photos, trips and places you want to visit. You see cafés and dinner tables with your favorite foods and culinary experiences.

As you look intently though this keyhole, you see everything you enjoy about life spanning as far as your eyes can see. You take a step back from the door and look for the key to unlock it, but you can't find it. You look around, you check your pockets, the counters, under the furniture cushions, but you can't seem to find it. Part of you feels like the key simply isn't there for you to find, so you give up looking for it. This is the metaphorical moment we decide to make the best of the happiness that we think is available to us.

You look around the room in which you're standing and

decide to paint the walls, get new flooring, get curtains, and create a happy home. You might even add some additional rooms to expand, or maybe a second story, and you start to be so focused on decorating and furnishing your home, and getting all the stuff that makes it look and feel great, that eventually you forget about that outside world. You don't see a point in looking for the key to access it because you are happy enough in your home on the hill, and you think it's good enough. When you get bored, you just redo your kitchen or living room or build another addition.

There's nothing "wrong" with making the best of what you have, but the problem with this scenario is that this level of happiness is not all that is available to you. There's that magical world out there, filled with true happiness, but that you no longer believe is attainable. But it is, and always will be. You just have to look in the right place for the key.

The key to true happiness is always within us. It rests deep within our true selves, which might have gotten a little buried along our journey of life thus far. There is a tool to quickly and easily find this key to unlock our true happiness—that tool is inspiration.

We do not need to settle for the happiness that we've come to know, expect and accept. Even when this happiness is "good enough," we always know deep down we are missing out on a deeper and more meaningful experience of life. The longer we prolong asserting that we deserve true happiness, the less attainable it seems, and sometimes we forget its possible.

The "pursuit of happiness" has become the equivalent of us decorating our life to be happy. The pursuit of happiness prevents us from experiencing true happiness. Until we decide to stop decorating our lives to be happy and let go of the happiness for which we have settled, we will be distracted from focusing on the real journey to the true happiness we desire and deserve. We'll discover how inspiration is the tool that will outshine the happiness we've settled for and take us directly to the true happiness within us that is waiting to be rediscovered.

♨

Happiness can be rooted in circumstances out of our influence, contingent on other people or attached to future events. "True happiness" can only be rooted only in our true selves, which is from where inspiration is inherently required to originate. We could call true happiness "inspired happiness," but for the sake of this book, we'll refer to "happiness" as the overrated happiness we've come to know, expect, and accept. We'll refer to "true happiness" as the unshakable, foundational happiness that stems from our true selves that is accessed through being inspired, leading us to live the inspired life.

"People may not be able to tell us how happy they were yesterday or how happy they will be tomorrow, but they can tell us how they're feeling at the moment we ask."[1]

—Harvard Business Review

CHAPTER TWO

Happiness Is Overrated vs. the Benefits of Inspiration

When you think about being happy, how does it feel? Light? Blissful? Easy? Relaxing? Maybe it's even a little breezy because happiness can feel like floating on a summer breeze that, unfortunately, can be swept away just as easily.

Now think about being inspired. You envision your favorite hobbies, activities, travel experiences or special moments. It doesn't feel light—it feels energizing! You experience vitality surrounding your awe of our world's most beautiful places or most interesting cultures, savoring taste-bud-tantalizing food, working on a craft project, expressing yourself through cooking a delightful meal or fixing up a classic car.

The light and easy feeling of happiness is not what makes happiness overrated. It's everything that happens before we feel happy that makes the reward of happiness overrated. We can spend hours, months or years waiting for happiness to kick in when we finally accomplish a goal or achieve a dream. With so much time, energy and worry needed to reach happiness, it's time we take happiness off its pedestal and replace it with inspiration. Inspiration produces immediate and enjoyable results without the wait and worry.

Let's look at some of the attributes of happiness compared

to those of inspiration.

HAPPINESS ATTRIBUTES

Calm energy, light, euphoric

Elusive—how do I get there and how long do I wait?

It's hard to choose happiness

Stimulates worry and self-judgment

Potentially rooted in external factors or people

Circumstantial

Potentially vulnerable when facing adversity

Feels like a break or vacation from reality

A pause on life's challenges

No release or change in stored negative energy

Temporary relief from stimulus and tangible energy

The voice narrating our every thought is in full effect

Focused on the "what"

Potentially contingent on uncertain future events

Loaded with expectations

Stimulates controlling behavior to ensure happiness

Easy and enticing to fake

Often ceasing with disappointment

Thought of as a destination (unrealistic)

INSPIRATION ATTRIBUTES

Energizing, feeling alive, feeling connected

Actionable—attainable right now

It's easy to get inspired

Does not induce worry or self-judgment

Rooted in our true selves

Intentional

Immune to adversity

Experiencing reality at its best

Recharging to lessen the impact of life's challenges

Cleansing, replacing stored negative energy

Infusing positive energy

The voice narrating our every thought has no role

Focused on the "why"

Completely in the present

Free of expectations

Controlling behavior is irrelevant

Difficult and unnecessary to fake

Ceasing feeling fulfilled and recharged

Thought of as an experience (realistic)

Let's explore the disadvantages of happiness and the benefits of inspiration.

THE PATH TO HAPPINESS IS ELUSIVE VS. THE PATH TO INSPIRATION IS IMMEDIATE

Getting happy isn't instantaneous. Sometimes it's a lot of work. Sometimes it's a lot of waiting or infinite waiting, or when we get happy, it's not what we expected. Sometimes we don't know where the path begins, how long it is or what's required. We all know what it means to experience happiness, but the path to it is elusive.

Happiness is overrated because we can want to be happy, but it's difficult to know what actions to take. Even if we create a roadmap to happiness, it can be difficult to take those actions. Even if we have taken those actions and finally achieve happiness, it's difficult to ultimately experience the lasting and fulfilling happiness we expect after such a journey.

Something that causes us so much concern, effort and stress, only to be repaid with an unpredictable and unsustainable outcome, doesn't deserve our energy and focus. We'll discover how inspiration is the most direct, actionable and enjoyable way to become truly happy.

Happiness Example: I'm not feeling happy. I need to feel happy. What can I do to feel happy? I'd be happy if I had more money or lost weight or had a better job. How can I do that? That's not possible in the foreseeable future. I guess I'll just wait for something to make me happy.

Inspired Example: I'm not feeling happy. I'm going to get inspired! I'm going to go on a walk in a beautiful park/enjoy a cup of something delicious/work on my craft project/read a great book/build something in my workshop/watch the sunset/savor my favorite food/do anything that inspires me, and I'm going to do it *right now*!

IT'S HARD TO CHOOSE HAPPINESS VS.
IT'S EASY TO GET INSPIRED

It's been said that happiness is a choice. So just choose happiness, right? For many of us, if we're feeling unhappy, it's hard to flip a switch and feel truly happy simply because we want to. While I strive for it, I have yet to genuinely live the "choose happiness" mantra.

Lucky for me, and anyone else who faces this same challenge, there's inspiration. Those that are truly happy didn't master the "happiness switch." The choice isn't whether or not to "choose" happiness, but instead to choose to live the inspired life with all of it's true happiness benefits. When we settle for the "happiness switch," we are focusing on a myth that is keeping us from the real tool to master: inspiration.

We don't need to judge ourselves or believe something is wrong with us because we can't instantly make ourselves happy. We can skip this whole unnecessary, worrisome and self-judgmental experience by simply getting inspired instead.

Happiness Example: I want to be happy. I'm just going to choose happiness! Hmm... I don't feel any happier... What am I supposed to do?

Inspired Example: I'm going to get inspired right now by taking a five minute break to enjoy something delicious.

HAPPINESS EVOKES WORRY VS.
INSPIRATION DOES NOT INDUCE WORRY

"Don't worry, be happy!" Oh, the irony. We worry about happiness. We worry about why we are not happy. When we are happy, we worry that it won't last forever. We hear that happiness is a choice, and we worry when we aren't able to choose it. We see other people who are happy, some with far fewer resources and some with perceived advantages, and we wonder what's "wrong" with us. We attach happiness to future goals, activities and outcomes. We attach expectations to happiness. We talk about "being" happy like we can make it last forever, when instead we watch it rush out as quickly as it rushes in.

We create a goal of happiness on which we judge ourselves if we struggle to reach this elusive destination. The more we practice worrying and judging ourselves, the farther we are from feeling truly happy, despite our best efforts.

We worry about happiness when we don't have it, but how often do we say, "I am feeling so uninspired. Maybe something's wrong with me. Maybe something's wrong with my life. Maybe I need medication."

We don't need medication to feel inspired because we know we aren't expected to be inspired 24/7. That limited duration is acceptable and almost earns more appreciation because it is so special. At the close of our inspired project or activity, we can simply seek or start another.

When you finish one art project or one hike or fixing up one car, you can simply start another when you want to. You always know you *can* and that you *will*, so you don't worry about it. There isn't a feeling of scarcity or concern when we aren't in a moment of inspiration because it's easy to get inspired. The benefits are instantaneous and you can take action immediately.

Happiness Example: I'm not feeling happy. What am I going to do? Something is wrong with me. Even if I was happy, I'd be thinking about how much I wish it would last forever because I know it's only temporary. I can't even fully enjoy being happy because I know the other shoe will drop eventually.

Inspired Example: I'm not even thinking about the fact that I'm inspired because I'm so present in doing what inspires me. I love doing this! I got so wrapped up that now it's past my bedtime. I'll come back to this tomorrow!

HAPPINESS CAN BE ABOUT OTHER PEOPLE VS. INSPIRATION IS PERSONAL

Inspiration is completely personal. That's why it's so gratifying! You can be inspired all by yourself and be totally fulfilled in that experience. Many of us inherently feel we must be loved and accepted by others to be happy, which are valid human needs. The trouble with these needs is they can negatively motivate us to hinge our happiness on other people.

Happiness can too easily be rooted in people, items and experiences outside our own influence. Chasing happiness through what we can't control is an exhausting effort.

We would never say, "Getting inspired is exhausting," because getting inspired isn't hinged on anything outside our sphere of influence, and it's easy and renewing!

Inspiration is everywhere if you're looking. The world gives us gifts every day. Vibrant flowers, eye-catching color, new music, tantalizing tastes, surprise rainbows, playful puppies—inspiration is abundant.

You may be inspired by all or none of those examples. The deeply personal nature of inspiration is what's so special about inspired experiences. Most people list similar "things" that would make them happy, but if you ask people what inspires them, you'll get a variety of different responses. By asking someone what inspires them, you'll discover their heart and soul. You'll see them light up and glow just by shifting your question toward the personal energy of inspiration and away from the wishful dreaming of happiness.

When you get someone talking about what inspires them, you can be sure you'll have a lively conversation that can flow for hours and provide an opportunity to truly get to know someone in a meaningful way.

Happiness Example: I'll be happy if I please my parents, but if I fail or if they don't care, I'll be crushed.

Inspired Example: I love camping! It's okay that my family doesn't like to camp, I still like camping just as much!

HAPPINESS STIMULATES SELF-JUDGMENT VS. INSPIRATION IS FREE OF SELF-JUDGMENT

We judge ourselves if we don't think we are happy enough,

which only serves to hurt our self-esteem, keeping us farther from our goal of true happiness. When we criticize ourselves, we further bury our true selves, and we can't experience true happiness until we uncover and connect with our true selves again.

We never judge what inspires us because it is the truest expression of ourselves. It's not even a question, it is truth. We might judge what makes us happy because sometimes it isn't based on our truth. Sometimes it's based on a quick coping decision, someone else's wants or needs, or anything else that doesn't reflect who we truly are.

There are two instances when we judge ourselves: 1) we are either judging the part of ourselves that is not in alignment with our true selves; or 2) we are judging the part of ourselves that someone else wants to change, and we aren't connected enough to our true selves to have the strength to ward off their judgment, so we turn it into our own.

That's why we don't judge ourselves when we're inspired—it stems from our true selves, that unshakable foundation of who we are that is not subject to judgment.

Happiness Example: I'm not happy enough. Something is "wrong" with me. Eating all that ice cream made me happy in the moment, but now I feel terrible that I made that choice. Now I'm really not happy.

Inspired Example: I delighted in every bite of that ice cream; savored the flavor and cool, creamy texture. And because I was present and tuned into every bite, I didn't need to over-indulge. I never regret doing anything that inspire me!

HAPPINESS IS VULNERABLE TO OTHERS' OPINIONS VS. INSPIRATION IS IMMUNE TO DIVERSITY

Happiness is too easily shaken when someone criticizes us. If we share happy news and someone responds critically or with judgment, we can't help but to feel discouraged, and our happiness can take a hit.

Inspired people pursue their inspiration simply because they can't imagine another path.

Consider someone who inspires you, who may have faced adversity, rejection and criticism and never gave up. It wasn't because they necessarily possessed more strength than anyone else, had "thicker skin," wanted it more, or had the ability or opportunity to try harder than anyone else. It was because their inspiration was genuine and an unstoppable force stemming from their strongest foundation. All the rejection in the world can't hinder one's desire to do what inspires them.

Inspiration is not about ego because the ego would be far too bruised by adversity. While facing adversity may be disappointing, it never stops an individual who is truly inspired.

Happiness Example: I thought I liked playing baseball until they made fun of me. Now I'm not going to play.

Inspired Example: I love singing! I'm disappointed that I didn't get the solo, but I'm never going to stop singing for me!

HAPPINESS ONLY PROVIDES A BREAK VS. INSPIRATION IS FULFILLING AND RECHARGING

Happiness is a break from our lives. Whether we've finished a bowl of ice cream or returned from a vacation, we come back to our life exactly as we left it.

Taking a break is not recharging. Our souls are not quenched by distractions or an escape from life's trials. We want to enjoy connecting and fully experience the connected moments that make us feel alive. We have to recharge and refuel to experience true happiness.

Humans are resilient. We can endure tremendous stress, be over stimulated all day, and then do it all again the next. But it isn't sustainable.

On a weeknight after an intense day of work, when reading may take too much mental involvement or it's too dark to take a walk, television can come to the rescue.

Screen time with television, videos or social media provide

easy access to decompression. But while screen time can be a simple and short-term option, it provides only a break rather than a recharge. We want a light distraction or a break from stimulus, but correspondingly, the recharge quality is as superficial as our experience of watching television.

During my 30-minute commutes to and from work, I like to learn a new language or sharpen my skills with instructional audiobooks. But when work is particularly taxing and my brain is maxed out, I have to give it a break. I don't even want to use my brain or listen to someone talk. I just want background music.

Brain breaks are important, but breaks are not enough to live the inspired life. Breaks are not refueling or recharging. Breaks do not connect us with our true selves.

The word "break" aptly implies that it's just a pause. Nothing is changing. Everything will be exactly the same once our break is over, though we may experience some short-term benefit from taking time for ourselves. We are looking to avoid activity because we literally need a break from stimulus, but the grind, the routine, the stimulation is still waiting for us. This pause doesn't help to exchange negative energy for positive refueling energy.

But what if we take more breaks? Do they compound to recharge us eventually? No. Breaks spent participating in energy-avoidance activities do not compound to become recharging because they don't replace or create positive energy. If we store stress, negative energy, or too much stimulus that is not in connection to our true selves, negative energy doesn't truly dissipate by taking a break. We have to move that energy. We have to replace that energy.

Since inspiration elicits positive energy through an experience or activity, inspiration is a powerful recharger. Participating in inspiring activities infuses positive energy, cleansing out any stagnation in its path and replacing dormant negative energy. When we take care of ourselves, we feel better about ourselves. Any kind of movement is a bonus because we are literally getting an energy flow going, cleansing out the old and replacing with the new.

Happiness Example: That vacation was great! I was so happy. But now I've come back to the same exact life! It's like I never left, and I'm just as stressed as before except I have more work to catch up on!

Inspired Example: That run was tough, but I feel energized less stressed. I can totally handle my big meeting tomorrow.

HAPPINESS EVOKES *THE VOICE* VS. INSPIRATION QUIETS *THE VOICE*

Inspiration quiets *the voice*. *The voice* is the chatter we hear that narrates every aspect of our day and conversationally shares the analysis about how we feel at any given moment—and it's completely unnecessary. We create it for one reason or another, but our true self knows what we feel and what we want without internally talking through it or about it.

Sometimes *the voice* is negative and judgmental about others or ourselves. Sometimes *the voice* sounds rational, but is really only a medium for doubting difficult actions that our true selves know are needed.

The voice is powerful and can shape the experience of our daily lives. It just keeps chattering away. But, when we are in an inspired moment, *the voice* isn't there. When we are truly present and captured by a gorgeous view, a perfect sip of coffee, shining the hood of our '57 Chevy, scoring the winning goal, or painting a compelling work of art, *the voice* doesn't have to narrate the meaning of that moment because we are present and acting in accordance with our true selves. Because we are so directly and deeply connected to our true selves, there is no translation time between what we know and what we think.

Meditation is built on "quieting" and removing *the voice*. If you have practiced meditation, you know that quieting *the voice* can be quite challenging, but it's entirely possible.

Happiness Example: Okay, I'm happy! This feels great. Oh no, I can't believe that just happened! Now I don't feel happy. How am I going to get that back? I could try this or that. I should do that. If I do, I'll surely get that back. But what if this happens? I should think about that.

Inspired Example: ... (I'm so inspired and present right now that I don't have to talk myself through what I'm thinking or feeling)

HAPPINESS IS THE WHAT VS. INSPIRATION IS THE WHY

Some of us think if we just had more money, then we would be happy. If we just looked a certain way or met the partner of our dreams, then we would be happy. And then what? "Happily ever after" turns into happy for a few minutes, a few hours, a day, a month, and so on. If we're lucky, we have a whole day of happiness until the crying kids, breaking appliances, and other challenges of daily life settle in to take over that "happiness" we worked so hard for. Happiness is fleeting.

Inspiration doesn't stem from classic forms of success, approval, validation, money or praise, but happiness might. While these aspects may seem motivating, they are often related to the "what" in the pursuit of happiness. And they happen to be irrelevant to inspiration.

The real question is *why* would you be happy about having more money? It's not the money itself, sitting in your bank, that's going to make you happy. It's *why* you want it, what you would do with it, and how you would spend it. The only way to make a decision on how to spend it is to tap into what inspires you.

If we live the inspired life, we are more mindful of the "why" and spend less time on the "what." Simply choosing to think about *why* we're working on a goal will bring us fuel while we're working on that goal, and we will not be holding our happiness hostage until we reach it.

Particularly when quitting bad habits or starting good ones, if we focus too much on the *what*, we might find ourselves spending too much time *thinking* about what we don't want and not enough time *living* freely in the flow of life.

What can we do instead? How can we NOT think of not smoking, biting our nails, eating that donut, or whatever we are working on? Focus on the *why*. We might want to quit a habit because we know it's healthier or we *should* (we'll learn more about those judgmental *shoulds* later). Reasons like this won't stand a chance once that habit starts taunting us.

Get deeper and more personal. Why do you want to stop doing what you're doing? Likely because you want something more meaningful than the vague reasons just mentioned.

We don't quit something until we are ready. It doesn't matter if we know how "bad" it is for us or that we or other people don't like it. If those were reasons enough, we would have stopped a long time ago. I have heard many smokers say "I'm going to die someday anyway, so what does it matter?"

While I may want to, there's no point in arguing, because even causing *a shorter life* isn't a powerful enough reason to stop smoking.

So how about living a *better* life? Get to those reasons. Do you want to be a better role model for your kids? Have you been avoiding a trip to Italy because you can't imagine going 14 hours on a plane without a cigarette? If you want to stop doing something, stop focusing on the *what* so much or you'll drive yourself nuts. Start focusing on the *why*, the part that is personal to you. Put pictures of your kids and Italy on your desk and as your phone background. The more you concentrate on the *why*, the more inspiring, powerful and supportive that *why* will become.

By age 15, I had been biting my nails for at least ten years. I hated it. I'd put tape or Band-Aids on my nails before I went to bed because I'd bite them so low that they were throbbing and the pressure of the Band-Aids made them feel better. One time I got warts all around my cuticles. They looked disgusting.

I tried that stuff that tastes bad to deter you from biting—I quickly learned to tolerate it. My parents would reprimand me or make comments. I didn't care. When I finally stopped, it had nothing to do with being sick of my bleeding, stubby fingernails.

I met and fell in love with my high school sweetheart and was dreaming about all the amazing things to come. I dreamt about my wedding and I wanted to have real nails. That's when and why I stopped the biting. I was inspired by how my wedding would be and that inspiration was enough to stop a bad habit I'd done for a decade and that no other conventional efforts could impact. While this reason might be ridiculously irrelevant to anyone else, certainly not worthy of someone else kicking a bad habit, it was the personal part of inspiration that gave it the power to change my life.

I turned the energy I used to put into biting my nails into inspired energy. I started painting my nails fun colors. I did fun designs. I painted different Christmas scenes with toothpicks on each nail during the holidays. I loved getting creative with my nails and taking care of them.

While I didn't marry my high school sweetheart, I did meet the love of my life more than ten years later, and I did marry him with my real nails.

It may take time to get to your true *why*, but it's your best shot at getting real and changing your life. Explore all *why's* and start to focus on them. Settle into the ones that make you feel something more than others. Continue to evolve them. Focus on your inspiration list, and you'll know when you're ready. It's your life. Let it be about your inspiration and no one else's.

I wish other people were enough to make us change, but generally, they aren't. Even our own lives are sometimes not enough. Wanting to be "happy" can be tossed aside so easily when it gets tough. "I'm happy enough, I don't really need to quit." Happiness is not powerful enough to break our habits, but inspiration is waiting, ready and willing. Inspiration is a powerful change agent waiting to be harnessed by you.

If you find yourself thinking about your goals, re-frame to think about *why* reaching these goals will bring you happiness, and you'll instantly feel the energy of tapping into what inspires you.

Happiness Example: I will be happy when I have more money. I want to win the lottery and be rich! I could buy everything I need to be happy!

Inspired Example: If I can get that work bonus, I'll be able take my kids to that cabin by the lake I loved as a kid. We can kayak and play games together. I want my kids to have special memories of family vacations the way I do.

HAPPINESS CAN BE ROOTED IN EXTERNAL FACTORS, OTHER PEOPLE, OR UNCERTAIN FUTURE EVENTS VS. INSPIRATION IS ROOTED IN THE PRESENT AND OUR TRUE SELVES

Happiness is generally quite conditional or circumstantial. "I'll be happy when's" rule our thinking, taking us out of the present and attaching expected outcomes based purely on hope. Even worse, the "I'll be happy when's" hold our happiness hostage from us for an unknown or even infinite period of time.

Attaching our happiness to outcomes we can't predict or control is giving up our empowerment over our own life. When we make happiness conditional and attach it to something in the future, we have to devise a plan on how to get there. Often, our plan takes time to execute—maybe *a lot* of time—and there are so many factors outside of our influence that can slow it down or get in the way.

If we don't seek greater connection to ourselves, the happiness closest to our fingertips will inevitably be impacted by changes out of our control. We'll be left confused, and maybe even lost, because our opportunity for happiness just went "poof" into thin air. When that happens, we make another set of "when's," plan another path, and start all over again. It's exhausting!

Don't settle for being happy *when*. Getting off this cycle is why re-framing to live the inspired life is so powerful.

Happiness Example: I'll be happy when I lose weight. (Until then, I'm going to hold my happiness hostage and criticize my body) OR I'll be happy if my love interest likes me back! (And if he doesn't, I'll be even more unhappy because obviously there's something "wrong" with me).

Inspired Example: I'm happy that I'm drinking this green smoothie and eating healthy. It inspires me to take care of my body, and every day I'm more inspired to keep making healthy decisions OR I'm happy and living my inspired life right now. If my love interest doesn't like me back, they obviously weren't the best fit for me.

HAPPINESS IS LOADED WITH EXPECTATIONS VS. INSPIRATION IS FREE OF EXPECTATIONS

Expectations are based on the future, which we can't control, and yet we can't help but hope to be the exception. We put expectations on happiness that often ensure we later experience disappointment. We expect happiness will make everything better. We expect if we can make someone else happy, that we will get what we want from them, like love, attention, or validation. We expect happiness to last so we don't ever have to be without again.

The expectations we place on happiness are simply our hopes. By setting an expectation of happiness, we are hoping the outcome will manifest exactly as we want it so we don't have to worry about or work to be happy ever again.

Maybe it's a new job, relationship, or new success, but when we put an expectation on happiness, we end up far more disappointed than if we just enjoy the experience for what it is in the present.

While happiness is laden with expectations, inspiration is free of them. The moment and the experience is enough.

We might say, "I hope [this activity] is enough to make me happy," but we would never think, "I hope [this activity] will inspire me enough." We never have to expect happiness or outline specific results from being inspired. We don't have to expect anything from inspiration because inspiration is always good enough exactly as it is, and it always serves us well.

Happiness Example: I thought when I got this new job, everything would be better, but now I'm just overwhelmed and my co-worker isn't interested in being very helpful. I really thought this new job would bring me more happiness!

Inspired Example: I'm so present in being inspired that I don't care how long it lasts. I don't need this activity to fix my life; I just need to enjoy it right now.

HAPPINESS CAN STIMULATE CONTROLLING BEHAVIOR VS. INSPIRATION ISN'T CONTROLLING

Sometimes, we want to "make" others happy to get what we think we need to feel happy. Making other people happy starts with the assumed feelings, needs and desires we assert on behalf of another. When we seek to make others happy, it's usually because we want their happiness to make us happy, to validate us, or to get attention. While these are basic human needs for children, as adults, we need to rely on ourselves to be our compass to happiness.

Making others happy so that we can feel happy means we are, perhaps unknowingly, making our feelings of happiness someone else's responsibility. Often times, they can feel we are trying to make them responsible for something that isn't their responsibility, even when we don't realize it ourselves.

In a worst case, yet common scenario, this pressure and unwelcomed need doesn't feel good and can result in resentment and the other person taking advantage of us, since we handed them control over our self-worth. As the cycle continues, if we don't get the reaction we were hoping for, we can get angry, sad or feel worse about ourselves. What a lose-lose situation!

Let's cleanse our palate of trying to make others happy. Let's let go of all that heavy energy of putting our self worth on the line, allowing someone else to determine our value. Seeking this method of being happy keeps us from getting inspired. Inspiration is not a tool to manipulate or get attention because we are so fulfilled doing what inspires us that we don't need anyone else to approve.

We accept inspiration as it is for what it is in the exact moment we experience it. We are free and letting life flow, and we don't even think about controlling the experience because it is so natural and enjoyable. We don't need to try to prolong it for fear of losing the feeling. We don't need to control other people to make our inspired moment more enjoyable.

Happiness Example: I would be happier if my partner gave me more appreciation. I don't really like cooking, but I think I'll go through a big ordeal and cook a big dinner! And if my partner doesn't appreciate it, I'll be so hurt and angry that I'll never do it again.

Inspired Example: It's okay if my partner doesn't like fixing up old cars. I'll work on my car on my own for a couple hours and then we'll get together after. I'll be in a great mood and in a better space to be a good partner after I spend some time doing what inspires me!

WE CAN TRY TO MAKE OTHERS HAPPY VS.
WE ARE INSPIRED FOR OURSELVES FIRST

We think about intentionally trying to make others happy, but we don't really think about intentionally inspiring other people. Being inspired starts with us, and if others also get inspired, that can be an exciting bonus, but we don't need others to be inspired.

Think about when you've been inspired by someone. Did he or she engage in their activity or cause to convince someone else or simply because they were acting authentically by speaking or acting from their true selves? Was this person's action driven by the need to impress other people or instead motivated by what they are passionate about? If you disapproved, would they have quit? If 50, or 100, or 1,000 people disapproved, would they have quit?

Inspiration starts with doing something we love so much that it naturally attracts others. Being inspired, ironically, doesn't stem from a strategy or need to influence other people, and yet inspiration can't help but inspire other people. Being inspired doesn't stem from low self worth or needing validation. It's fueled by the strength, conviction and certainty of one's true self. It's genuine from where it originates and how it's shared, and it's equally genuine when others respond by being inspired.

When someone gets inspired by you, it is pure and without motive. Just like when you are inspired and share that feeling. Your true self has connected with another's true self through shared inspiration, and this creates one of the most moving and powerful connections possible.

Happiness Example: The person I'm dating likes to cycle. I bet if I start posting content about cycling on my Facebook, they will like me more. I bet if I take a picture with my friend's bike, they will think I'm their perfect partner!

Inspired Example: I love cycling! It was on my bucket list to cycle across the United States, and I just did it. I just got 5,000 followers? I wasn't even paying attention! Did I just inspire those people? That's awesome!

IT'S EASY TO FAKE HAPPINESS
VS. INSPIRATION IS SHARING OUR TRUE SELVES

An important aspect of humanity is that we want to be

seen. By seen, I mean seen, heard and recognized by others for our truest selves. This means we have to put forth our truest selves. It means we can't hide who we are, lie about how we feel, or suppress real emotions, even when it's unpopular or others don't like it.

It's so easy to fake happiness, and it's often subtly encouraged. When we are at work, we have to put on our best face in front of our boss or customers or clients. When we are in social settings, we don't want to be the one bringing everyone down. On social media, we must be sure we are sharing our happiest selves.

There's not much room for us when we aren't feeling happy. If we fake happiness for too long, not only can it start to feel normal, but it continues to push us farther away from our true selves.

When we seek to be inspired, we do so holding ourselves in high regard, honoring the importance of our needs, desires and inherent rights to a positive life experience. We deserve to be inspired, and when we're struggling, we don't have to *fake it until we make it*. Instead, we can get in an inspired moment. We can get inspired in a small way or a big way. It's really easy to fake being happy. It's really difficult and unnecessary to fake being inspired.

We either are or aren't inspired. We're not a little inspired or "kinda" inspired. We are inspired, uninspired, or the topic or experience is irrelevant to us. But happiness? We can be a little happy or a lot happy, but there isn't a definitive threshold of being happy or not being happy. It's easy to fake or lie about being happy. Being inspired is concrete. That's why it's so easy to jump into it, even for a moment, and really feel it and mean it.

Being inspired is the healthiest route to being seen in the way we all crave and deserve because it is natural and authentic. The authenticity of passion that comes from creating art, overcoming obstacles, and the genuine joy we naturally express when being inspired is so easy to tap into and share.

Happiness Example: My partner loves this movie. I better laugh at the parts they laugh at. I wish I was watching anything else. They're looking—I better smile!

Inspired Example: I love cooking! I don't even think about pretending because I'm too busy julienning this bell pepper. This is going to be delicious!

HAPPINESS ENDS IN DISAPPOINTMENT VS. INSPIRATION ENDS IN FUFILLMENT

When we're happy, we don't want it to end. Of course we don't! But this sets us up for disappointment.

Inspiration, on the other hand, has a built-in end, so your expectations are set accurately from the beginning. You know there will be an end to your ride, project, meal, and so on, but because you know there will be an end, you are more in the moment and less concerned about how long it will last. In fact, you're probably not analyzing it at all because you are so present in the moment. You might even celebrate the end of being inspired as an accomplishment, whereas with happiness you may find yourself unfulfilled and disappointed.

Happiness Example: I've had such a tough week. I think I need a shopping spree to feel better! I'm so happy I bought all that stuff I wanted! Except I don't really feel better now and I racked up my credit card. I guess that shopping spree wasn't enough. I don't know what will ever be enough.

Inspired Examples: 1) I just finished that book and it was *so good!* I'm still thinking about the plot twist. I'm going to tell my friend how good that ending was!

2) Wow, I just finished that race! I feel so alive! I'm going to go celebrate! I'm not even thinking about if or when I'll do my next race because I feel so fulfilled by that experience!

THE PURSUIT OF HAPPINESS KEEPS US FROM EXPERIENCING TRUE HAPPINESS

The most overrated quality about happiness is that it is distracting us from the inspired path to the true happiness we desire and deserve. Now that we've exposed that happiness, as we know it, comes with many side effects, let's learn about the antidote with which to replace it in order to live the truly happy life: the power of inspiration.

"I confess I do not know why,
but looking at the stars always makes me dream."

—Vincent van Gogh

CHAPTER THREE

How Do You Know if You're Happy or Inspired?

Up until a year ago, I had never run a continuous mile. In high school physical education classes, I was always one of the last three people to cross the finish line. I never understood why it was so hard for me, and I grew to hate it.

More than twelve years later, I felt running calling to me. I felt it summoning me like truth from deep inside my soul that I needed to break that barrier—or at least try. I set out to just run a little at a time... like 30 seconds, followed by walking for a minute or two. At the age of 30, I ran my first full mile without stopping! Eventually, I was able to run two miles. My pace was slow, but I couldn't believe I had actually *run*. I might even be a *runner* by some standards.

BEING INSPIRED IS NOT THE SAME AS BEING HAPPY

Running did *not* make me happy. I felt miserable the entire time. Every part of my body and mind was confused by why I was torturing myself. So if running didn't make me happy, and I didn't have an affinity for physical discomfort, why was I running? It wasn't easy or enjoyable, but it was invigorating and meaningful. I ran because I was inspired.

Inspiration defied my normal behavior and choices to avoid physical discomfort. I was trying something new, breaking down barriers, challenging myself, and creating new personal records with the energy of inspiration surging through my body to tell me to keep going.

After breaking for winter, I picked up running again a few months into the next year. I was nervous about what the experience would be. What if I lost "it"? What if my experience the previous summer was a fluke and I really can't run?

I set out and fairly easily ran a mile and a half. My pace was slow—it's possible you would have out-walked me—but I was inspired by my surprising success. Two runs later, I covered 2.5 miles, my personal record for my entire life. And I didn't hate it! I wouldn't say running makes me happy, but it excites me. It makes me feel alive. It taps into a part of my true self that I had hidden for a long while.

BUT ICE CREAM MAKES ME HAPPY!

When I need a pick-me-up, I always turn to ice cream. Please feel free to replace your favorite go-to food for this example.

If I'm having a tough day, I might be ready for half a carton of ice cream to make me feel happy. I think this experience is affectionately called "eating my feelings." I might feel happy while I'm eating ice cream, but I'm not going to feel happy after, and I won't feel inspired at any point!

Ice cream provides me the temporary happiness we've come to know, expect and accept, which also means a happiness that melts away as soon as I put the spoon down. I won't be fulfilled even after half a carton, and likely I'll have a stomachache of regret. All that and I'm still not truly happy.

So ice cream does make me happy temporarily, but it comes with all the side effects of being emotionally unfulfilling and being uncomfortably filling in my stomach!

Here's the twist—depending on *how* and *why* I choose to eat ice cream, it can also inspire me. We can tell the difference in our activities between being fueled by inspiration (motivated from our true selves) and being driven by the pursuit of happiness (motivated by who knows what).

How do we eat when we're inspired? Slowly, savoring each bite. Exploring every detail of the flavor experience. What else are we doing? If we're inspired, we aren't doing anything else. We aren't eating mindlessly while we watch television or play with our phones because we are completely present enjoying the experience, whether intentionally or naturally. If we are enjoying our food with a friend, our conversation might slow a bit or be about how absolutely amazing the edible experience is. Everything falls away when we are in inspired moments, setting the stage for exclusive personal delight.

What's the test of a great meal? When dinner is served and everyone becomes quiet. That's unmistakably inspiration at work! How much do you eat? Do you just keep going and lose track? Or do you have a reasonable serving and end up being even more fulfilled than you would with twice as much if you were feasting in a pursuit of happiness?

These questions illustrate the fundamental difference between how we feel after pursuing happiness (disappointed that it's over) and how we feel after being inspired (fulfilled and recharged).

Whether it's ice cream, a new project, listening to a favorite song or a reading a book about something we care deeply about, we don't finish feeling unfulfilled if we are doing so from the source of inspiration. We finish feeling more energized and motivated.

Use the "ice cream inspiration test" analogy to identify the difference between when you're inspired and when you're pursing happiness. You can use how much you lose yourself in the experience and how you feel afterward as a mile-marker to help you choose inspiration more often.

OTHER EXAMPLES

I can have music on in the background or I can jam out to my favorite song. I can have the radio or a playlist on and be happy enjoying it, or I can intentionally seek energy, solitude, comfort, motivation, consolation, empathy from music. When "my jam" comes on, I will likely interrupt you to tell you that this is "my jam," and you might lose me for three minutes while I rock out and enjoy it.

Listening to music to make us happy is a completely different experience than when we become inspired by music, and there's likely a good time and place for both. Music provides us a great example of how we can engage in the same experience from either the foundation of happiness or inspiration, and how the source of our choice creates a different experience during and after.

You can drink coffee, or you can be inspired by coffee. You can grab your coffee and go, rushing between meetings or you can indulge in being inspired by the smell, the taste or the start of a new morning before everything else rushes in.

You can cook a quick meal on a Monday night or you can cook an inspired meal, selecting the best ingredients, tinkering with the flavors after each taste test until it's just right.

You can hike a mountain and tromp swiftly to get to the top, or you can enjoy the journey and be present in every aspect of your surroundings. You can be inspired by the flowers, views or sounds of nature.

There is nothing "wrong" with doing any of these activities in an uninspired way. The purpose of highlighting these differences in how we choose to engage in these experiences is to outline that we *have* a choice, not to judge which choice we make.

If we are looking to use inspiration as a tool, we can activate it by starting to consciously choose to engage in inspiration more often.

STEP 2:

Discover the Power of Inspiration

"If you want to discover the true character of a person, you have only to observe what they are passionate about."

—Shannon L. Alder

CHAPTER FOUR

Three Inherent Prerequisites to Inspiration

While happiness feels light and blissful, inspiration feels energizing, focused, empowering, exhilarating, challenging, creative, driven, or stimulating. When we are inspired, we feel alive, free and connected to our true selves.

Being inspired is a form of authentic positive energy and emotion felt immediately as we indulge in and celebrate what we love and enjoy about life. Seeking inspiration is a much easier and actionable choice than trying to choose to "be happy." Living the inspired life means you'll seek inspiration and you'll attract inspiration. Before you know it, inspiration will surprise and delight you everywhere, and you'll find yourself living your inspired life.

Inspiration gives us confidence because it can't be judged. When we share our inspired selves, being authentic and vulnerable becomes easier and being truly "seen" becomes possible. And being truly "seen" is the only way we can be truly loved.

There are three attributes inherently required to feel inspired: being connected to our true selves, acting in honor of our true selves, and being present.

BEING CONNECTED TO OUR TRUE SELVES

The only source for true inspiration is our true selves. When we are connected to our true selves, we don't doubt ourselves. We aren't unsure about what we feel or what we want or what we like or what we don't like.

Connecting to our true selves can be challenging for many reasons; We may be too "in our heads" from a really focused day or month (or year) at work; we may have sacrificed self-care and inspiration for too long and are having a tough time getting back in touch; or we may have had childhood experiences or relationships that taught us to hide our true selves. When these challenges linger for too long, we can forget how to re-discover our true selves.

We have to be connected to our true selves to live our lives authentically on the path that speaks to our deepest wants, needs and desires. If we are feeling inspired, it is our true selves shining through in pure self-expression. Feeling inspired is our glimmer of truth and self when we've lost that connection.

When I found myself among the wreckage of a soul-jarring breakup, I felt like I didn't know who I was. I just lost myself in the relationship, and without it, I didn't know how to move forward because I didn't even know what direction forward was. I didn't realize that I had buried my true self, the compass of my life, so deeply.

I felt like a sailboat that had been shattered by a storm, my scattered pieces of wreckage floating along wherever the waves wanted to take them. Parts of me floated in separate directions and in every direction. I was moving, but not as a whole person. Different parts of me floated to where it seemed they were needed to keep some kind of motion or to stay afloat, but I wasn't navigating.

Throughout my life, up until that breaking and waking up point, I didn't know myself well enough to realize that I wasn't connected to my true self. And I certainly wasn't empowered enough to feel I had the ability to lead or create my life.

I had to heal the reason I got so disconnected and fragmented in the first place. I had to reclaim my pieces and mend them back together. I had to reduce the distance between fragmented parts of me and my true self so that I could become whole.

The ocean, like life, always has movement. A sailboat with all its parts together, in its wholeness, can lead it's own way, cutting through challenging waves with strength, ease, purpose and determination, no matter the pull and push of the waves.

We face challenges pushing and pulling us in a million directions all the time, whether we're being pulled to hide our truths or pushed to compromise our integrity. The more we are connected to our true selves, the more whole we are. The more whole we are, the stronger we are to navigate our own life.

We get whole when we start collecting and reclaiming those estranged pieces. We get whole when we know what to do with those pieces because they are all aligned in purpose with our true selves' desires, wants and needs. We get whole when we let our compass be the only compass that guides our life and when we don't stray because the winds of other people's opinions, wants or needs are trying to blow us off course. We can get whole by rediscovering our true selves, most easily accessed by allowing ourselves to get inspired.

ACTING IN HONOR OF OUR TRUE SELVES

Inspiration is the most radiant and flourishing expression of our authenticity. Because inspiration is deeply personal, we honor our true selves through the simple act of being inspired.

If we aren't connected to our true selves for any reason, we can be superficially happy about a lot of things. We can even be happy about things that make others happy.

While superficial happiness may seem good enough, it keeps our true selves at bay. It reinforces that we think we aren't worthy of enjoying deep and meaningful happiness because we don't feel we're good enough to show or share our true selves. When we choose to act in a way that does not honor our true selves, we are letting ourselves believe that someone can better live our lives for us. The more we allow it, the more we believe it.

Alice Miller, from her book, *The Drama of the Gifted Child: The Search for the True Self*, mentions the "tragic and painful state of being separated from his true self, to which doctors refer offhandedly as depression."[1] Denying our true selves is a common cause of depression and unhappiness; inspiration can provide opportunities to accept and share our true selves.

The most important needs of our internal human experience are to be seen, loved and accepted for our truest, most authentic selves. In order to experience these, we must honor and share our true selves to experience the purest form of these basic human needs.

When we are young, we seek approval from our parents. We compromise our integrity to fit in with new friends. We seek these needs in the easiest way we know how, which often results in temporary and superficial happiness.

Much like settling for happiness, when we settle for love and acceptance that is based on conforming or manipulating ourselves, it further disconnects us from our true selves and reinforces that we should continue to hide who we really are.

As children, the common desires to be seen, loved and accepted can train us to sacrifice ourselves to obtain them. As adults, it's our job to course-correct to be seen for who we truly are in order to experience true love, true acceptance and, ultimately, true happiness.

The journey isn't always easy, but inspiration is the quickest shortcut to discovering and practicing embracing our authentic selves.

BEING PRESENT

Being inspired inherently requires being completely present. When you are enjoying your favorite coffee, witnessing a breathtaking view, mountain biking on your favorite trail, or about to cross the finish line in your first marathon, you are completely present. Everything else fades away. You literally cannot experience true inspiration if you are not completely present in that moment.

Being present leads to a healthier mindset for many reasons, including reduced stress, reduced worrying and greater acceptance of our true circumstances so that we can face them and move on.

Comparatively, if we're focused on what's next, what could happen, or those "I'll be happy when's," we are missing the opportunity to connect with ourselves, be fulfilled and be inspired in the present moment. Living by the "I'll be happy when's" can unnoticeably become an excuse to defer dealing with present circumstances or to defer self-acceptance.

As we know, happiness is a break from the present and inspiration is immersed in the present. When we are inspired, we experience authentic joy, elation, freedom, and self-expression. Inspiration is how we both completely lose and definitively find ourselves in the present.

*"[Inspiration] will help dissolve your perplexities and purify
your character and sensibilities, and in time of care and sorrow,
will keep a fountain of joy alive in you."*

—Dietrich Bonhoeffer

CHAPTER FIVE

Inspiration Saves Lives, Happiness Doesn't

No one says, "happiness saved my life." Thousands of people can say, "music saved my life," "cooking saved my life," or "sports saved my life."

Inspiration keeps kids who are on the edge from falling off. And inspiration is accessible to anyone. It costs very little, or nothing, for parents, mentors and friends to share inspiration around, for example, music, cooking or sports. Unhappiness is a symptom of problems many young people face. Inspiration saves them—it offers them something productive to pour their time into, it allows for opportunities to build self-esteem and achieve goals, and it creates an empowered desire to change their circumstances and realize their dreams. Happiness simply doesn't do that.

Happiness feels like a privilege to struggling kids, but inspiration feels like home. The same can be said when we struggle as adults.

MUSIC SAVED MY LIFE — LOUIS' STORY

Louis was 14 when he had his skiing accident. Living in the German Country side, he skied every day there was snow and skateboarded every day there wasn't. He also took drum lessons, but that was just "for the girls." Most of all, he loved sports, being outside and active.

One cold day in February 2009, Louis decided to finish his day of skiing with a more adventurous run off the beaten path.

On the untouched side of the mountain, snow was generous with deep layers of fluffy powder. It was so deep that Louis fell, losing his ski's, which disappeared easily into the fresh snow. As he began sifting around to find them, the change in the snowpack triggered an avalanche. Louis was swept up and pummeled down the hill, past boulders that would have killed him, only stopping his momentum when his body wrapped around a tree.

He was airlifted out and induced into a coma for two weeks while undergoing many operations to repair broken bones and assess a spinal cord injury.

"When they woke me up from the coma, I didn't even know I had a skiing accident. I couldn't move anything below my chest and my right arm was mostly numb. I could only feel my bicep, thumb and index finger."

Louis thought he would be walking out of the hospital in three months, but that wasn't the case.

"I asked my doctors when I would be able to walk again. They said, 'you're never going to walk again. You're paralyzed now.' That was the moment I realized that this was going to be really tough. I was 14; I had my whole life ahead of me! I knew it would be a lot of work, but I was not going to accept that my paralysis would never get better."

Louis' dad invited many experts to help with different kinds of therapies and treatments, including "thought training."

Intrigued, Louis started working with his thoughts. He'd start the day saying, "Today is a good day. I'm happy."

"I'd say I'm happy 200 times a day. I was just lying there for hours telling myself positive thoughts, and it *did* help. Then I realized the power of using my thoughts, and I started researching it. I decided to get the feeling in my fingers back."

For hours every day, Louis would look as his finger and tell himself he could move it. He started ergo therapy for his hands and was offered a piano for fifteen minutes a day.

"I could only hit one note at a time, but it felt so good. It just felt right."

When he would play, he imagined the sound resonating through his body with healing vibrations.

"The doctors were always so negative, but I pretended that the music and sound waves would heal me."

After two months of his imaginative piano playing and concentrating on moving his fingers for several hours each day, a finger finally started to move.

"I saw it move just a little. Maybe the first time I just imagined it, but it was incredibly motivating for me! I did it! The doctors told me I wouldn't move my fingers, but I never stopped believing I could do it. I just knew I could."

It took one and a half years to get all the feeling back in his right arm and fingers.

"I believe it was a combination between not giving up on my intentional thought therapy and my piano therapy."

After he was released from the hospital, he moved in with his dad in Munich. He had to go back to school a few days a week. He never liked school much, but now he really didn't want to go.

"You go from a hospital where everyone is struggling with something or are in a wheelchair like me, and then back at school, I was the only one in a wheelchair."

His dad bought him a guitar, which is how Louis spent his

time at home.

"People would say it helps to write down your thoughts, but it was so hard for me. But when I picked up my guitar and started playing chords, then I could write. "

Louis' dad provided encouragement and resources to do a great deal of physical training and healthy eating.

"It was intense. It was too much for me as a teenager. So when a friend of mine moved to Portugal and asked if I wanted to come for a few months to learn English at an international school, I knew I wanted to go. They were really good friends with my parents and they promised they'd take care of me. The house and school were wheelchair friendly, and I needed some levity to break free from the intense daily pattern of my life."

Louis ended up staying in Portugal two years to graduate from the international school.

"I was never very motivated to go to school, but for some reason I really wanted to learn English. Portugal was perfect. I made a lot of friends there and it was always sunny. We had a pool, and I swam every morning and got back into a more balanced healthy lifestyle."

One evening in Portugal when he was 16, Louis played some of his original songs at a party where famed British songwriter and record producer, Mike Myers, was among the guests.

"He saw how people responded to me on stage and invited me to record in his Portugal studio. Mike got me into music even more. He showed me how to use the programs and how to record properly. We only recorded one song, but I learned so much."

Today, at 21, Louis is one of four students welcomed to attend his dream school, Zurich University of the Arts.

"It's the best school in Europe to learn music composition for film, which is what I enjoy the most."

Louis has his own own studio now, limitless in what he can

create.

"Without music, I have no idea what I would do. My every day is infused with music. Either I'm scoring for film, playing the piano, listening to music, composing electronic music or singing with my guitar. Music makes me feel alive and represents so much of who I am today."

During our entire interview, Louis is glowing with positivity and true happiness. Music is Louis' way of expressing and sharing his true self. Music created an opportunity to be seen not as someone in a wheelchair, but for the talented musician and powerfully positive man he is.

Louis' strength, attitude and presence is inspiring. Music has become Louis' outlet for his true self and a conduit for the surge of inspiring energy and life itself.

I asked for Louis' advice for anyone working on overcoming a challenge.

"You need to want it 100%. You need to be convinced that you will be able to do it, that you will make it, and you need to work so much with your thoughts. Physical therapy was helpful, but for me, I attribute 90% of where I'm today to how positively and intentionally I use my mind to create my thoughts."

His advice is to never give up, but it didn't mean he didn't have times of doubt and discouragement.

"Of course, many times I thought 'I'm done, I'm in this hole and I don't want to do this anymore.' I thought that a couple times a month. But it's not how often you think that, it's the thoughts that we choose after.

"I would tell myself, 'you're not done, you're so happy. You're so happy to be alive! You're so happy that you can move your fingers! You're so happy that you can play music! You're so happy that you have people that care about you. You live in Munich, you have everything. Don't mess it up.'

"It's important to recognize how happy we are, even if we have a challenge like being in a wheelchair. It's all in your head—everything starts in your head. Someday, you will move your fingers, or reach whatever your goal is, but it will take time and it will take effort. You need to take the risk. I still do it. I've been looking at my feet for four years, concentrating on getting them to move, and I still get nothing."

Four years without any reward for his effort? I asked how he stays so positively committed:

"I just know that it's going to work out at some point. I just know it. I don't know how many more years it's going to take me, but I'm not going to give up. By thinking positively, so many great things have come into my life. It's like a magnet. If you think positively and you act positively, positive things will come to you. The same is true if you think negatively about your life, then negative stuff is more likely to follow."

He says that, in his greatest times of struggle, music helped keep him inspired and positive.

"You need to find something you love, whether it's cooking, making music, drawing, building something or collecting little trees," he laughs playfully, making me curious if he actually collects little trees. "You have to find something you love that inspires you and focus on that."[1]

COOKING SAVED MY LIFE – BRIGITTE'S STORY

Brigitte Thériault first felt love from her grandmother's cooking. Her father was an alcoholic and her mother was in survival mode, neither able to be very present in her life. Brigitte doesn't have too many memories of being with her grandmother, but she remembers it being the only time in her childhood she felt taken care of.

How does a 14 year old become a stripper? "I was dating someone whose 18 year old sister seemed to have what I wanted. She was beautiful and making ends meet to raise her son. She seemed so strong and was making her life work on her own. I told myself that I want to be like that, and therefore, since she was a stripper, I would be able to do it through being a stripper, too. I figured once I turned 18, I would be able to have that option. I started to plan on stripping as my solution."

Any solution seemed better than her present circumstances.

"At that age, I was searching for love, connection and a sense of belonging. My dad spent his days drinking Molson Canadian beer, and our dilapidated, filthy, smoked-filled farm house made me feel like I constantly had dirt crawling under my skin. The combination of these things, along with my grandma, the major loving figure in my life, dying when I was 13, destroyed my ability to feel anything but anger and resentment."

When Brigitte met someone who was going to a strip club, she asked to come along. She walked right in at age 14, and they didn't even ID her. The next time she went, she walked into the dressing room and onto the stage."

For the next few years, Brigitte made her money stripping. She started dating someone when she was 17 that had a "real" family.

"He had a father and mother and two brothers. They had a nice home and they spent time together in a way I'd never experienced.

"His mother was the classy, nurturing French lady who, despite working in upper management, still made meals from scratch for her family. Her cooking changed my life. It was not only her delicious food, but the beautifully set table, the candles, the wine, and the family discussion that made me feel like a cultured woman and not a trashy stripper. I fell in love with how good fancy home cooked food made me feel so connected and alive."

Brigitte started using her money to eat out at the row of Little Italy restaurants in her hometown of Ottawa, Canada.

"Restaurants filled my desire for deeper connection and pleasure. They were my first foray into becoming a cultured and civilized human."

49

She started cooking at her boyfriend's house with his mother. She began cooking her way into a new life of savoring, entertaining and creating.

"I loved cooking for other people, sharing what I loved with them. I saw how food connected people, and creating what inspired that connection finally made me feel alive.

"I quit working at the strip club and moved to Montreal. The food scene was culturally diverse and rich in flavor."

Two years later, Brigitte saw an ad in the paper for cooking school, and she knew she was going to enroll.

"That year of cooking school saved my life. I discovered who I was as I discovered the craft of creating inspiring flavors to pair with inviting presentations. I found freedom to feel alive for what made me *me*. I could finally feel, because what I had to feel was finally positive. I felt a true sense of hope and connection to life and a way out of a destructive past."

After cooking school, Brigitte prepared to move to New York. To afford her dream, she placed an ad to trade housing for live-in cooking duties. She met a father who had recently lost his wife, and home cooked meals were just what he and his young daughter needed.

"I no longer had to stay numb to live. Cooking brought me to life, and gave me the power to live authentically, inspired, and holistically fulfilled."

In New York, she started her own personal chef business, White Apron, and carried it to the West Coast. Brigitte also teaches aspiring personal chefs, and her next dream is to take her family on a bus to eat their way around the United States.

"My recipe for relationships has transformed as well. I know what it is to love and be loved by people who treat me well. And my first love has become a life-long passion that nourishes me. Today you can find me in the kitchen creating new recipes, teaching clients how to cook, and feeding the people in my life. My love affair with food will never end, and I am grateful to have found a passion that took me out of an existence that might not have had such a happy ending."[2]

COOKING SAVED MY LIFE – RONDA'S STORY

Can you imagine knowing that at any given minute, you could go blind? You could walk to your bed at night and wake up paralyzed in the morning? Multiple Sclerosis (MS) is one of the most unpredictable diseases that literally can steal critical bodily functions overnight, and you always know that this moment or the next could be the last time you see your favorite view or can do a little dance in the kitchen to your favorite song while cooking.

Ronda Giangreco's life changed overnight when she woke up one morning with half of her body numb. Thinking she had a stroke, she was told to take some aspirin and get to the doctor right away.

When the second half of her body went numb, they had to look at a different diagnosis—Multiple Sclerosis. Even more heartbreaking, her husband's mother had passed away from this same disease, and fear overtook them both as they realized that "this was it." At age 53, Ronda was given a poor prognosis for mobility. Ronda asked herself, "If I only have a year left to walk, where do I want to walk to? What do I want to do?" The answer for Ronda was to cook.

She asked her husband how his mother coped with this disease. He said every week his big Italian family would get together for Sunday dinners. They would load his mother and her wheelchair into the car and go to his grandmother's house for a family meal. They would eat and laugh and share stories and enjoy wine. It was something to look forward to each week and they made memories with every bite.

That's what Ronda wanted to do. She had attended cooking school twice in Italy and she decided to try her best to cook an Italian meal every Sunday for one year.

During that year, Ronda had a lesion that caused acute severe pain attacks. She would be rushed to the hospital and be

51

dosed with something to sooth her screaming pain. This happened one Sunday before she even made it to the store to shop for that evening's dinner.

She told herself, "This is my own private Mt. Everest. Every week that I get dinner on the table, I am farther into triumphing over this disease's prognosis." And she did complete 52 Sunday dinners. She always had six guests, whoever were first to RSVP. Sometimes she asked neighbors she didn't know. One time, she invited someone she met at the grocery store.

"It wasn't the cooking or the food itself, it was bringing people together. It was breaking bread together. The first fundamental need we have and our first opportunity to be nurtured is around being fed. It's our first opportunity to feel loved and cared for, and that tradition extends to a dinner table in our adult life.

"The goal wasn't to keep myself out of a wheelchair. It would be ridiculous to say I could cook my way out of this." Ronda just wanted to live as whole-heartedly as she could one week at a time. "Hosting the dinner parties was something positive I could focus on. Choosing to create and live in each inspired moment as it was happening gave me something good out of something so bad. If I had set out with a goal beyond just living whole-heartedly through those 52 weeks of hosting Sunday dinners, it would have fallen so short of what I could have lived up to. A goal I could have imagined would have limited my potential. I never would have set the bar as high as it went. I just wanted to have some positive and good in all this craziness."

As the weeks went by, even through her intense pain attacks, each Sunday dinner helped take her focus off her disease and place it on her triumph.

Ronda didn't have any expectations about what would come of the commitment she hoped to fulfill. She hosted her dinners to have those experiences in those moments, and that was enough. She didn't think beyond the commitment or try to strategize what might result. Ronda's desire to be inspired through cooking and hosting these dinners led to a life that was happy and fulfilling; one she wouldn't have dared of with her diagnosis.

I asked Ronda what would have happened that year if she hadn't set out to make those 52 dinners. "I think I would have given into it. When you get a disease that can be so debilitating and challenging, you get tremendous sympathy. It's seductive. Nobody faults you for sitting on a couch and eating a tub of ice cream. Nobody expects anything of you. If I hadn't expected anything of myself, I think I might have succumbed to that seductive sympathy and the low bar that had been set for me."

It wasn't cooking that saved her life. "It was the inspiration that saved my life. I am lucky to be able to walk and cook while living with MS, and I am grateful to have been inspired, to have allowed this disease to be a reason for me to rise instead of crumble."

After her incredible feat of hosting 52 Sunday dinners, folks would hear her story and encourage her to share it. She wrote her first book, *The Gathering Table – Defying Multiple Sclerosis With a Year of Pasta, Wine & Friends.*

Ronda had always dreamed of writing a book. When she was twelve, she would dream of seeing her book in a bookstore window—a towering display right out of the movies—creatively stacked with the cover prominent and one with the author portrait revealed.

In high school, she was voted "Most Likely to Write the Next Big American Novel." But as life moved on, she got a job, got married, had kids, and lived a "normal" life. Her dream of authorship got buried under the life that was expected of her.

It rained torrentially the evening of her first book signing at her local bookstore. Even as she was on her way, she questioned, "Who would come out on an evening like this just to hear me?" Under pelting rain, she and her husband approached the front door of the bookstore, and then she saw it—the book display she had always dreamed about.

"It was like I was 12 again. I just stood there in this rainstorm and sobbed." After taking in the experience in, and getting quite drenched in the process, she saw, beyond the book display, sixty eager readers waiting to welcome her. Ronda, indeed, was now an author.

This wasn't an end; it was just the beginning.

When Ronda was diagnosed with MS, she wanted to stop. If she was on a path from A to B, she didn't want to be on that path. She didn't want to move forward because what was she moving towards? "I never thought dreams or goals would ever be part of my life again. Boy, was I wrong!"

Ronda now since published her second book, *A Dose of Devotion – How Couples Living with Multiple Sclerosis Keep Their Love Strong*, co-authored with Jeanne Lassard. Ronda has spoken all over the United States and realized dreams that would have never been fulfilled if she had never been diagnosed with MS.

The worst experience of her life is responsible for her fulfilling her greatest dreams. "Even if I woke up paralyzed tomorrow, I would say it was all worth it."

"Don't wait for life to shake you into pursuing your dreams. Don't wait for a wake up call, because it may come too late. Live the inspired life today, because you don't know what tomorrow will bring.

"I don't know why I got lucky, but I feel a great responsibility to do everything I can to help others."[3]

BASKETBALL SAVES LIVES

Basketball is of particular interest as a source of inspiration to kids of all ages, ethnic backgrounds, financial means and even physical capabilities.

In the inspiring article, "Basketball Saved My Life" by Paul Brown[4], Paul shares the perspective of Lance Haggith, a UK basketball coach honored with BBC's Sports Personality

Unsung Hero award in 2010, who dedicates his life to acting on the knowledge that basketball "can really change lives."

Haggith creates basketball projects through his charity, Sports Traider, and says he's seen a decrease in anti-social behavior.

"That's because the kids are out playing basketball instead of out on the streets. They put on a shirt and feel part of a family, a family they may not have at home. Their gang is the team they play for—not the gang that's waiting for them out on the street.

"I've even worked with young offenders, and playing basketball has helped stop them from re-offending.

"They actually serve as good role models for some of the other kids because they provide a reality check. Their experience proves that going to prison is not a badge of honour."

Basketball doesn't cost money to play, making it accessible. "I've seen kids who can't afford their own shoes take a pair off when they leave the court and give them to the next kid."

It's not exclusionary, because you can play even if you're in a wheelchair.

"Quite simply, basketball is a sport which is open to everybody. It's not elitist in any way."[4]

BASKETBALL SAVED MY LIFE – CONNER'S STORY

Continued from the previous article[4], Conner Washington, a UK Basketball Star, lost his parents when he was just a child.

"Losing a parent at such a young age was beyond anything you could imagine. I lost the most precious gift in my life.

"It would have been so easy to lean towards negative behaviour in order to cope, which could have been anything from taking the drugs route, being violent, or crime.

"But the most powerful feeling that protected me from not breaking down was the incredible desire I had to make my mother proud of her son. It's because of her I chose to channel my broken feelings, discovering a saviour that has essentially saved my life.

"Basketball became my guardian angel personified. I became so fascinated with all the tricks ball players could do with the ball. I was obsessed with the elegancy with which they could execute movements, which looked almost choreographed.

"The entire style of the game lit a flame inside of me and that flame is still burning bright to this day."

For Conner, and all of us, inspiration is a powerful flame that, once lit, can provide light for a lifetime.

BASKETBALL SAVED MY LIFE — DAWN'S STORY

In the article, "'Basketball Saved My Life,' Says New RRHS Coach"[5] by William Wilczewski, Dawn Myers, a female coach, shares that basketball became an opportunity to share her appreciation for the sport and to inspire other young players.

"Honestly, I had a rough family life growing up, and if it weren't for basketball in high school, I really don't know where I would've been. I tell [the girls I coach] every day basketball saved my life because it kept me in the classroom and it kept me safe and off the streets ... so I wanted to kind of give back to these girls what my coach gave to me."

SPORTS INSPIRES ME TO LIVE FULLY — XERXES' STORY

Xerxes Whitney has run marathons, climbed mount Whitney, coached collegiate and high school tennis teams, meditates, writes poetry and is a middle school physical education teacher. He is an accomplished athlete who's been active in and inspired by sports and the outdoors his entire life. He also was born with cerebral palsy.

"Being unique isn't easy," Xerxes, pronounced Zerk-sees, shares. His speech is slowed and seems to take effort. He walks a little funny and sometimes his arms probably don't behave exactly as he'd like. He is a good looking guy. But I know all of these surface representations are not what Xerxes, or anyone, wants to be *seen* for.

Cerebral palsy affects body movement, muscle control, muscle coordination, muscle tone, reflex, posture and balance. It can also impact fine motor skills, gross motor skills and oral motor functioning.

How could this man, with a diagnosis of cerebral palsy, excel more than most through sports and physical activity?

"My parents didn't treat me any differently than my siblings. Getting food on the table was a bigger challenge than my disability."

His parents tried to enroll him in horseback riding when he was young, but it just didn't inspire him.

"I wanted to play baseball, so I did. My grandma got me tennis lessons when I was 13, and I fell in love with tennis."

He didn't have many people to practice with so he would hit hundreds of balls a day against a wall. He ran cross country in middle school and played tennis for his high school team all four years.

What should have been one of Xerxes' biggest challenges served as his greatest inspiration.

"I liked that sports were black and white. I either caught the ball or I didn't. So I just kept practicing and I kept getting better."

Xerxes went on to play tennis in college, also getting his Bachelors degree in Economics. His team finished second in the country four years in a row. He ended up being a collegiate tennis Team Manager and Assistant Coach.

"I dreamed of being a collegiate tennis Head Coach. I felt discriminated against when I didn't get the position with the tennis and coaching experience I had. Not getting that job was the first time I really felt like my disability kept me from a dream.

"I had a vision that only I could hold my own self back, but when I couldn't get hired or the girl I liked didn't call me back,

I was at a dead end. I didn't know how to navigate that."

Missing out on the coaching position, he got his Masters degree in Applied Sports Science. Even a Master's Degree wasn't enough to make landing a job easy.

"After a long, drawn-out job search, I started working for my dad. It was definitely a low time in my life.

"I had a resistance against explaining that I had cerebral palsy because I didn't want to be defined by cerebral palsy. I want them to see *me*. I thought if I didn't talk about it, then it wouldn't be an issue. But the less I talked about it, the more it was an issue."

The discouraging job search provided a set back that felt new to Xerxes. He discovered poetry and began expressing himself through writing. Through poetry, he felt free to bear who he was and he wasn't afraid to share how he felt.

"There is no greater freedom than actively being true to who you are."

He got a job as a high school Athletic Director. He decided to get his teaching credential, and joined a middle school as their Physical Education teacher in 2000. He's been teaching at the same middle school ever since.

"I would be so positive at work all day, feeling great about making a difference and really living my life, but then I'd come home and be alone. I got inspired to get to know the relationship with myself no matter what feeling I'm experiencing."

Xerxes discovered meditation, which helped him more deeply know his true self. Through meditation, he began shedding layers of heavy emotions. He began attending meditation retreats, some local and one 10-day retreat in Thailand.

Not to leave any stone unturned, Xerxes also decided to climb Mount Whitney.

"It only seemed right given my name. It wasn't easy, and it really tested my balance, but I felt so alive on the mountain. I felt how fleeting life could be because I knew if I slipped, I could be gone.

"During the ascent, I started think about how I've always been really focused on achievement. I've always felt like I was supposed to accomplish a lot. The desire for achievement pushed me toward goals, but it always left me feeling unfulfilled. I was running marathons, but I realized I could always run faster, no matter how fast I ran. There was an emptiness accompanying always trying to prove myself.

"When we got towards the top, my friend and mountain climbing partner said, 'we have one hour to make it to the top—should we go for it?'

"I knew I was slow and tired, and in those moments of internal conflict, I realized that I didn't have to get to the top to feed that need for achievement. I didn't need to prove myself anymore. We turned back, and I started really embracing the journey instead of the destination."

Meditation and poetry continued to inspire him along his journey of self-acceptance. He released his first book of poetry in 2002, entitled *What's Your Name*[6], a tribute to his struggle and acceptance of his complicated name and the challenges he faced pronouncing it when he first met someone. He released his second book, *Busting Through: Exploring My Truth*[7], in 2007.

Xerxes continues to tap into what inspires him to keep his students motivated and inspired.

"I've probably given a few hundred high fives in the last two days," he says, fresh into a new school year.

When I asked if the kids are tough on him when they first meet him, he replied, "They just want to know if it's going to be a cool class. If I'm showing that I'm comfortable, then they can be comfortable with me. Sometimes meeting kids is easier because they don't have a story behind what makes me different. They don't have a story of how it should be. As adults, we build up limitations. To my nephews, I'm just their uncle."

I wish I could say that inspiration empowered Xerxes to make his biggest dreams come true and made his cerebral palsy irrelevant, but this has yet to prove true.

Inspiration has, however, kept Xerxes living a vibrant, healthy and happy life despite his disability. He encourages his students to be positive, infusing meaningful quotes into jumping jacks and daily exercises. He inspires other through sharing his story and poetry.

"If tomorrow is my last day on earth, I want to know that I've given all that I can, that I've had the best experience of life attainable, that I've lived authentically and that I've made a difference."[8]

ART SET ME FREE — LORENZO'S STORY

Lorenzo's upbringing was very sheltered and fear-based. Growing up with low self-esteem and in a rural area, he was shy to say the least. Through adolescence and high school, he was "fearful of everybody and everything."

"My mom would say, 'go play with the kids,' but I didn't want to. I was just a hermit in my own way. I lived in a small farm town with a lot of machismo and not much sensitivity. I felt imprisoned. I felt like I wasn't allowed to be who I truly was inside."

Lorenzo experienced his first glimpse into being inspired to reach for more out of life when he was inspired by two people: Bono, from the band U2, and a psychology professor.

Bono sparked a creative outlet for Lorenzo. "Bono was so insightful and inspirational with his charisma and big ideas. He wrote some of the most powerful poetic lyrics, and it made me want to do the same."

Lorenzo began exploring poetry as a new opportunity for self-exploration and self-expression.

He met his next mentor in his first year of college when he took a psychology class, prompting new ways of thinking to which Lorenzo had never been exposed. Initially, different ways of thinking and ideologies felt like a foreign intruder on the norms by which he felt tightly contained as a and child. He started to realize that if everyone else was so different, maybe he would be allowed to be different, too.

"My psychology professor was uniquely supportive. He invited every student to his office, not to talk academics, but to meet each of us 'as a person.' I thought that was awesome! He wanted to meet the real me, and so did I. He was a stepping-stone for me. He coached me to not be afraid of who I was and encouraged me to explore my poetry."

Later in college, Lorenzo reached a new low. A deep depression drove him to leave the group dorms for a solo room instead. He started skipping classes.

"I was grappling with a lot of shame, always thinking I wasn't good enough. All that messaging was so strong. I just stayed in my room. I didn't talk to anyone for long periods of time. I was very afraid to share any part of myself with anybody, thinking that I had no value in doing that. I never put myself out there, I never ventured, and I never tried anything."

Fortunately, there was one class that revealed that a more accepting and expressive environment was possible.

"There was one program at Sonoma State University called The Learning Community, which was the least academic course they had. In class, we spent several hours a day sitting in a circle. The instructor was there, but not instructing. We all just talked, and we created our agenda as we talked. We shared whatever we wanted to share. It was very open ended. This was the start of feeling comfortable being me and thinking maybe I could share who I was. Even if I wasn't actually *that* different, I still perceived I was."

Lorenzo started to realize that he was the only person holding himself back from expressing his true self and being seen.

Then, he met someone he really cared about. He started to feel safer opening up, but only a few short weeks later, he found himself broken-hearted.

"She broke up with me and I was devastated. It wasn't about

how much time we were together, but about how much I committed and finally felt ready to open up. I had a wake up call that I didn't need to take care of myself through someone else. Someone else didn't have to be that piece of me to fill my void. *I* needed to be that piece of me. I realized I had to give myself the love that I needed. What I was doing wasn't working and it wasn't giving me the life I wanted. So I started working from the inside out."

With a newfound determination to start taking care of himself, Lorenzo filled that void he'd had for so long with *himself*, not through anyone else. And that's when he met his wife, Michelle.

"Before it was 'want, want, want, want,' and then I let it go. And then the love of my life walked into my life so effortlessly. We connected, and still do, through the essence of who we are as individuals. Our connection blew my superficial checklist out of the water! She introduced me to yoga and meditation, which I still practice to connect with myself and tap into my creativity."

Lorenzo started to share himself more freely, but it wasn't until art became a part of Lorenzo's life that he fully experienced freedom.

His friend created a replica of a painting by artist Drew Brophy.

"Drew's art really spoke to me, and I looked him up. The more I discovered his work, the more I felt inspired. It all really connected with me."

Lorenzo decided to go to Southern California to an open house Drew was hosting.

"It was so inspiring to meet Drew. He is a surfer, an artist and he loves nature. That's who he is and what he does. His confidence was so infectious. He lives outside the norm of how people make a living. Here's this person confidently living his dream, and he made that seem normal. I felt connected to how Drew was sharing his energy through his work."

Lorenzo got inspired to do his own painting and re-introduced "Patches," a character that had surfaced during an art therapy assignment in college.

"Patches shows who he is, and he is vulnerable. He shows his heart, showing it's okay to connect. I forgot about him. Then when I got inspired to paint, he came up as something to expand upon.

"He's multicolored and looks like he's patched up, which represents a double meaning for me. The different colors represent my appreciation of diversity and how multidimensional and multifaceted we all are. The other meaning is the visual representations of how we have to patch ourselves up through tough times. He represents healing."

The following year, Lorenzo went to Drew's open house again, this time with a canvas and a dream. "I had the idea of Patches surfing on one of Drew's classic wave depictions."

Lorenzo was honored and ecstatic when Drew agreed to collaborate.

"Drew has thousands of paintings and he's a world-renowned surf artist. He is so inspiring to me, and *he* agreed to collaborate with *me*?! It was powerful." Even as Lorenzo shared his story, it still strikes a deep emotional cord of meaning. Today, he has the collaborative piece, entitled *Wave of Inspiration*, sitting on his desk.

For Lorenzo, before tapping into self-expression and connecting through art, everything was linear. Rules gave him predictability and safety. Through art, he discovered freedom, confidence, and an infinite scope of possibilities.

"Art has been an avenue of unspoken connection of my true self and another's. Drew and his wife, Maria, have been so supportive of my journey with art and sharing my voice through painting. The encouragement I've received from them is not the kind of messaging I received as a child. Connecting through art has brought healing and given me freedom to express myself."

63

He is inspired by witnessing others in an inspired moment.

"I love watching the unveiling of something soulful and being able to recognize and appreciate it. It's like I'm in their world for a little bit, and it feels so special and so important. It feels good to be trusted with that and to be supportive when someone is sharing their true selves."

Lorenzo believes being inspired "makes life worth living."

"I get to bring this character to life that I've had inside all these years. I get to put him on a canvas. It's exciting to have a visual way to share him, and essentially, fearlessly share myself."[9]

STEP 3:

Discover What Inspires You to Re-Discover Your True Self

"To be yourself in a world that is constantly trying to make you something else is the greatest accomplishment."

—Ralph Waldo Emerson

CHAPTER SIX

Discover What Inspires You

The journey to discovering what inspires us is also the journey to connecting with our true selves. As we discover new inspiring experiences and even re-discover old ones, we are making it easier and faster to connect with our true selves. The more we're inspired, the more we practice tapping into our true wants, needs and desires. We gain confidence in the natural self-expression reflected by being inspired.

Inspiration can be a fun part of your journey in discovering your true self as you learn more about what you personally enjoy, what excites you, and what brings you energy.

MAKE YOUR INSPIRATION LIST

Making an inspiration list is an engaging way to begin focusing on inspiration and discovering what inspires you. Our inspiration list is our go-to when we need a boost of inspiration—a menu of sorts—especially if we're having a tough day and need a reminder of the activities we can engage in to lift our spirits and get refueled.

I co-created the ub:inspired app to encourage and assist people in joining and creating groups that capture all that inspires them. It features a digital inspiration list, but paper or another type of digital list will work well, too.

Take at least five minutes to think about experiences that bring you positive energy and make you feel alive. List everything and anything that you enjoy, from five-second experiences to your favorite travel destinations. List tastes, smells, songs, sounds, activities, places, and moments. List free experiences and expensive experiences. List experiences you've had and experiences you want to have. List tangible and intangible things.

List the little things, like a beautiful view or lilacs or the smell of cinnamon. List the big things, like where you want to travel, where you want to live, and what you would do with more money (the inspirational "why"). Things you photograph or want to photograph. Give yourself plenty of room to explore everything that inspires you.

Keep your inspiration list top-of-mind and have fun with it! Add to it the minute you think of something new or when you find yourself in a surprise moment of inspiration!

You'll find that once you start looking for inspiration, it will be abundant in your life. By giving up the quest for happiness and focusing on inspiration instead, your mind will be active, your heart will be full, and your soul will be nourished.

MAKE YOUR GOAL LIST

Goals keep us inspired when we are connected to what our true selves authentically desire. Our goal list will be shorter than our inspiration list because we want an abundance of what inspires us and we only want goals that we truly want to actualize and will work towards. If we have too many goals or our goals are more what we think we should do rather than what we truly want and are ready to change, our goal list can negatively serve as "proof" that we can't progress. These goals are not helpful and can do more harm than good to our self-esteem and quest to connect to our true selves.

Pairing goals with inspiration is a powerful combination. Our goals provide ongoing engagement and focus, keeping us connected to ourselves. When we add a variety of inspired moments on top, we create magical momentum in our lives.

Pair your goals with a description, paragraph or story about the *why*. If you make a goal to buy a house, it won't be as meaningful without the *why* or the purpose. Whether you want to learn something new, overcome a challenge, run a marathon, finish a project or lose weight, include and focus on the *why* and how it feels to be inspired while you're in the experience of working toward your goal.

For example, if your goal is to buy a house, focus on why you want to buy a house. Some *why's* might include to have your own creative space and would you do within it, to paint or decorate rooms the way you like, to someday have a family, to have a garden, to take a step of independence, to be able to entertain friends and family, to have a kitchen you can cook in, to have a backyard you can relax in, to have a backyard for your kids to play in, to create a feeling of home for yourself or your family, or whatever else resonates with you.

Most of us would agree that a goal to have $1,000,000 is a desirable one. But if we won't be making an executable plan to help reach that goal, it instead belongs on a wish list. Wish lists are not included here intentionally. Goals on wish lists start from what we want to happen *for* us, not from action we will take to actualize our dreams. We want our goal list to include only items we are empowered and ready to actively pursue and achieve.

STAYING PRESENT IN YOUR GOALS
Goals keep us fueled, inspired, active, focused, and anticipatory. Goals can be powerfully positive and motivating, but also laced with negativity if we aren't careful. They can

indicate that something better is in the future, but we don't want our goals to discourage us from feeling fully empowered to live the life we want today. If we aren't meeting a goal on the timeline we hoped or expected, we don't want to invite shame, self-judgment and low self worth on our journey.

These challenges present opportunities to be resilient—to not put all the "I'll have my perfect life" eggs in a single metaphorical basket. So what are healthy goals, and how do we have a healthy relationship with goals? Dream big, but give yourself room.

I have learned that I have an unrealistic sense of my abilities. My default sense of my ability to "make things happen" if I try hard enough is more delusional than not. However, this generally has served me quite well. Once I was able to shed some layers of dysfunction I'd collected and take the reins of my own life, I grew to be bold, brave, and ask for what I want. And simply by asking, I have a decent rate of success. But the times I gave my all and still couldn't control a favorable outcome felt utterly deflating. Like something was wrong—with me, the world or justice itself.

We may never explore the depth of our potential without dreaming big, but we can never fully control an outcome. We can only influence it. As Wayne Gretzky said, "You miss 100% of the shots you don't take." It better serves us, as kids or adults, to sincerely believe we can do and be anything we want to. If there's any take away, it is to find a way to believe this so whole-heartedly that we never shy away from our biggest and boldest dreams because of fear, vulnerability or possible "failure."

Equally, we must not allow goals to stop us from being present or allow the "I'll be happy when's" or "I'll have the life I want then's" to play a role in our journey.

So how do we avoid the "I'll be happy when" mentality? Let inspiration be enough. Live the inspired life now, and don't make happiness contingent on something out of our influence.

If we eat well and stay active, we'll lose weight, but it's hard for anyone to believe that our body is "perfect" or exactly as we want it to be. If we're making inspired decisions, we'll feel good about ourselves, regardless of details related to "perfection."

We can let our goals motivate and inspire us, but we don't want to let them determine our happiness or self worth. We could take acting lessons for years and years and still not get the coveted lead role. It doesn't mean we're not good enough. It just means it wasn't the best fit based on someone else's subjective decision. We continue acting, or whatever your personal equivalent might be, simply because there is no other alternative. We love it, and it is an important part of who we are. Our goal might be to get the lead, but we continue living the inspired life regardless.

MAKE YOUR BUCKET LIST

The bucket list is everything you want to do during your time on earth. Bucket list items are our big ticket inspired experiences for which we may have to save money, carve out time, or both.

The foundation of the bucket list is the least present because we are looking at something we perceive to be years or decades away. The foundation of a bucket list isn't the dreamy part of it, it's the choice. Just like the difference between our goal list and a wish list, bucket list items still require intention, planning and commitment to follow through.

It's okay to dream about your bucket list, but don't let it stay a dream. Can you check off a bucket list item at least every one or two years? Only you can make it happen, and you deserve to check everything off your list.

By having your inspiration, goal and bucket lists, you'll have fun crossing off completed items and discovering new ones. You'll be discovering and connecting with your true self, creating positive and refueling energy, and creating inspired momentum that enlivens every cell in your body.

"We become what we think about.
Energy flows where attention goes."[1]

—Rhonda Byrne, The Secret

CHAPTER SEVEN

Use Inspiration to Change Your Life

SEEK INSPIRATION

Just like the law of attraction and the power of intentionally practicing gratitude, the more you focus on seeking inspiration, the more abundantly it will be present in your life.

When starting ub:inspired, I sought to practice the lifestyle we were hoping to promote. We began our quest by waking up at 5am a few days each week to head to a local nature preserve to watch and capture time-lapse photos of the sunrise. We also sat out on a high school football field to observe a meteor shower in the middle of the night. Neither activity was conducive to our preferred sleep schedule, yet I felt more energized afterward.

I started to look for opportunities in the world to capture inspiration, and it was as if the world stepped up to give me the best. Beautiful flowers popped up everywhere. Random acts of kindness seemed free flowing. A double rainbow appeared directly in my path driving home on the drab, backed-up freeway. Everything seemed more inspiring, and leaning into inspiration became so easy and enjoyable.

Since being present is a prerequisite for being inspired, I naturally was present so much more. I went on an inspiration photo hunt, seeking to capture anything and everything that inspired us. I got bold with seeking new and different experiences in nature. My then-husband and I hiked to the Sykes Hot Springs in Big Sur, California, for a day trip. We started our hike at 6:45am, and didn't get back until 9:15 pm that night.

While we may have underestimated the time it would take to complete a 20 mile hike, our late arrival was partly because we were so captivated by inspiration. For the first three hours of the hike, we were so inspired by gorgeous views and beautiful flowers. Their perfect water drops and inviting colors begged us relentlessly to be photographed.

Being free to stop, enjoy and capture these moments instead of stomping by with only the destination in mind brings our bodies, souls and spirits to life. These moments are what we most remember about that day.

There are eight concrete ways to use inspiration to change your life. These will take mindfulness, intention and follow-through, but will prove infinitely rewarding.

1. TEND TO AND GROW YOUR INSPIRATION, GOAL AND BUCKET LISTS

Your lists will be your guide along your path of inspiration. When life takes over, we can come back to our lists to find something to get us re-inspired and re-focused on what we love most about life.

Check in on your list items and keep them top of mind. You don't need to be actively working on all of your goals; just put energizing momentum into at least one. Actively work toward at least one bucket list item, even if it's still a year away.

Researching what's on your bucket list can be fun and inspiring, too!

To keep your lists top of mind, you can use ub:inspired or make a photo collage. Find creative ways to surround yourself with your list, and keep adding to it.

We deserve to be inspired, and we must choose to not allow daily life to become more important than making time to indulge in thinking about and acting in inspiration.

2. TRY SOMETHING NEW

Inspiration surges when we try something new. When we try a new food, whether we love it or don't like it, we still feel inspired. Not only do we feel more adventurous and interesting, but we are discovering ourselves with every bite. By knowing additional information about what we like and don't like, we are furthering our connection with and understanding of ourselves. There's so much we can learn about ourselves that we can never know unless we try something new! It seems simple, and it is! It's a fun and easy shortcut to getting to know your true self. How often can you try something new?

Try a new dish at your favorite restaurant or try a new restaurant. Try a new recipe at hope, or a new spice or sauce. I thought I hated curry most of my life and now it is one of my favorite dishes. Try Frisbee golf, a new trail, or be a tourist in the next town over. Try a new body wash scent, a new color to wear, or paint a new color in your room. Try a new scented candle or car air freshener in your car. Even the smallest adventures in trying something new can change your day. How often can you try something new by challenging or delighting your five senses and experiencing new activities?

3. LEARN SOMETHING NEW

Learning something new is a larger commitment than trying something new, but it offers lifelong benefits. Whether you want to learn a language, a new cooking skill, a new hobby or a new sport, learning something new keeps our brains active and our inspiration piqued.

We feel good about ourselves when we can do something we previously couldn't. We have the opportunity to connect with a new set of people who have learned what we are learning, whether in person, in digital communities, or years later when we can reflect upon it.

Not only is the experience of learning inspiring, the results are fulfilling. Love the Italian language? Learn it and add "Visit Italy" on your Bucket List. Always been inspired by amazing photos? Learn the art of landscape photography and add "Photograph Zion National Park" to your Bucket List.

What would you normally pay someone else to do for you? Learn how to build a Wordpress website, fix a leaky faucet, work on your car, make gnocchi, or feng shui your home.

Learn about how things are made, why there are different varietals of wine, read about history or learn how to make a cartoon version of yourself in Adobe Illustrator. Tutorials and information are abundantly at our fingertips, especially on Duolingo, Lynda.com, and YouTube.

4. FOCUS ON THE *WHY*

We've covered the purpose of focusing on the *why*, so now we have to practice it. If we want to lose weight, we have to connect with something deeper than being able to fit in our desired pant size. If we want to stop a bad habit, we have to focus on more than simply not doing it.

Make a vision board (or use the background on your phone) for the *whys*. We can put up photos on our desks or nightstands about the *why* to remind us. Consciously choose to focus on the *why* when you find your mind obsessing about the *what*. Eventually, it will become a more natural way of thinking, and you'll feel intrinsically motivated from the inside out.

5. NO MORE "I'LL BE HAPPY WHEN'S"

Decide not to entertain "I'll be happy when's" any longer. When we find ourselves allowing a person, event or outcome to hold our happiness hostage, we have to literally catch ourselves and decide to accept ourselves as we are.

If you notice yourself thinking an "I'll be happy when," replace it with something inspiring that brings you to the present. Make your experience of life about the journey, not the destination.

6. LEAD DECISIONS IN YOUR LIFE

No one can run your life better than you, but if we're not feeling confidently connected to our true selves, we might feel otherwise. Instead of leaning on others who are willing to lead our lives for us, we must do our own personal work. To lead our lives, we must know ourselves well enough to know what we want and we might have to learn or enhance our skills, whether critical thinking skills, how to cook or how to fix a running toilet.

Leading our lives might also mean saying "no." If we're not accustomed to it, saying "no" can be hard, and it's okay if we start on small things. We have to practice saying "no" when we want to say "no" until it becomes comfortable.

7. PRACTICE CHOOSING INSPIRATION

We know from the "ice cream test" that sometimes we can do the same activity from a source of pursuing either happiness or inspiration. We have to practice choosing to get inspired until it becomes our natural default.

Sometimes, we'll have to choose to make time for inspiration, but more often than not, we simply need to choose to upgrade our existing activity to one that is more inspiring.

Here's a story about how one reluctant choice helped me get back on track.

A GLASS OF WINE VS. THE TREADMILL

During a stressful period of my life, I came to enjoy a glass of red wine a few nights a week after work. Because I was working my day job and coming home to an evening of building my business, I needed something that was just for me. I didn't think I could afford a break, much less an inspired recharge session, but I needed both.

I could drink my glass of wine while I worked from home. I could offer something enjoyable to myself without having to really break or recharge. Though I limited myself to only one glass, I wasn't a fan of using alcohol for stress relief or a coping skill.

I knew that many new business owners work two jobs to get to a point of transition, but there was just *so* much to do. Any time I took a break, it felt like a setback from my goal. I was willing to sacrifice a balanced life, in the short term, in exchange for building the life I really wanted in the long-term.

The problem was that I was unhappy and it showed. It showed in my internal daily experience, in my relationship, and in my day job. I knew I was disconnected from myself, and it wasn't getting better. I was always in overdrive and couldn't "soften up." I was so in my head that I couldn't tap into my heart. I wasn't the warm, loving person I normally was.

I was strategic and productive and making things happen, but that's the only way I could operate. Even if I could have tapped into the "soft" parts of me, what if I couldn't get back to that uber-focused, out-of-my-way-I'm-getting-stuff-done me? I might lose effectiveness and time! And it was only temporary, right? Just a few months—maybe three or nine or twelve. I accepted it had to be that way for the time being. I could get through this temporary period in exchange for the lifetime of happiness I was pursuing, right?

No, I couldn't. I was watching the "me" I knew and loved get more buried every day. I was so analytical and calculated. I felt robotic and became uncomfortable around the people that knew me as a human. Sure, I was getting so much done, brainstorming impactful ideas, and being a great resource. But I was also increasingly unhappy. And then I received unequivocal proof that I had to change something. I stopped fitting into my pants.

My new coping skills were starting to show on my hips, and I either needed to buy a new wardrobe or a treadmill. Since the price would have been about the same, I opted for the healthier, sustainable solution.

I got a treadmill off Craigslist for $300. I decided to do 30-45 minutes of exercise in the morning. While I knew this choice could only provide benefits, I was surprised by the results:

1) I was less stressed at my day job when I began my day with movement and time for myself. I watched a show on the iPad as I exercised, so I got a break and distraction from my regular environment (resting my brain). Combining a brain break with getting inspired through strengthening my body and seeing of what my body was capable created a perfect combination to starting my day happy and recharged.

2) I stopped wanting wine. When I exercised, the last thing I wanted was a glass of wine after work. I just burned 300 calories! I'm not wasting that on wine. And because I've already taken time for myself that day, I don't come home feeling oppressed by self-induced demands that I once felt were required to perform my day job and build my business.

3) I fit in my pants. After exercising in the morning, I didn't want to waste my effort by eating all the goodies in the office or coming home to that glass of wine. With an improved diet and exercise, I lost the few pounds I needed to stay in my current wardrobe.

4) I was happier. I felt better at work, my relationship

was definitely better, and I felt better about myself. I was more in alignment with the needs of my true self. My ambition no longer talked me out of allowing the basic self-care I needed. While I was still putting in at least 30 additional hours a week working at home, that little break in the morning made the time at work more enjoyable.

There were a number of benefits engaged by my choices. I was recharging every day, giving myself more inspired and happy fuel to get through my day. I was cycling out the stress and negative energy and replacing it with feeling good about taking care of myself. I gave my brain the break it needs from the "go-go-go-do-more" track. Ultimately, by "sacrificing" 30 minutes a day, I leveraged 24 hours of feeling happy and inspired.

We go into overdrive too often, and our health and happiness depend on us being able to do more than simply going through the motions. Refuel with inspiration at least once a week when you are in a busy spell. You'll leverage and create more benefits than what you sacrifice.

It's important to have breaks, but they will not protect us from carrying stress in our bodies and they will not give us the access to connect deeply to our true selves. Give your soul a surge of inspiration and you'll connect with why you do what you do all over again.

8. PRESCRIBE INSPIRATION & TAKE YOUR DOSAGE

Being unhappy, you might say, "Why am I not happy? Maybe something is wrong with me." Being uninspired, "I'm not worried about not being inspired because that isn't scary and certainly doesn't mean something is wrong with me." We don't take Prozac when we aren't inspired.

What if, when we are feeling less than happy, we were prescribed two genuinely inspiring experiences each day?

Required, doctors orders. Let me state clearly that I am not qualified, nor do I intend to take an anti-medication stand. There are many medical conditions rooted in physical causes, which can impact our state of mind. What I will assert is if any individual is able to connect to what inspires them, it can only have a positive impact. Inspiration can still help anyone struggling with happiness.

I do believe that, from time to time, most of us need something to make difficult changes easier to move through. That "crutch" might be in the form of a supportive friend, a therapist, a medication, a vacation, or a personal day. As long as the crutch isn't harmful to you or anyone else, then why not give yourself a break? The ultimate intention is to live an inspired and happy life where crutches aren't needed, and weaning off that crutch is certainly easier with inspiration as a tool.

WHEN WE DON'T CHOOSE TO BE INSPIRED

Inspiration is everywhere, and it's up to us to focus on it. Media today is littered with dark aspects of humanity, whether through news stories about local and worldwide tragedies or sarcastic talk radio or podcasts focused on negativity. If you can't do something to change what frustrates you, why indulge in it? How is it serving you?

Sometimes we indulge in these experiences because we can connect to existing feelings we hold of anger, resentment or negativity. It makes us feel okay about those feelings, but it doesn't help us change those feelings. It perpetuates a negative story we tell ourselves about people, humanity, circumstances, our world. It potentially keeps us in a victim mentality or, ironically, making us feel powerful over these circumstances as we further reinforce them. What we focus on perpetuates, and we always have a choice.

These negative occurrences are happening whether we focus on them or not, and the same is true about inspiration. Inspiring people, stories and events are out there whether we seek them or not. Choosing to seek inspiration can be much more uplifting and so much more fun! Your choices create your experience of life, so why not choose to be inspired?

"You don't have to see the whole staircase,
just take the first step."

—Martin Luther King, Jr.

CHAPTER EIGHT

Change Your Life One Inspired Moment At A Time

I remember one day looking at my front yard, full of weeds, and feeling completely overwhelmed (a feeling enhanced by really not wanting to face this chore). I wanted to cry, actually. I had bought a big house, I was engaged at the time, and then quickly separated. Now this yard was a big symbol of how I have to do "it" alone.

The weight of that truth was extremely heavy and brought on many emotions. I avoided the weeds until they became too much to ignore. I didn't know at the time that this front yard of weeds would serve as an important healing experience.

ONE AT A TIME

An epiphany dawned: How do you remove a yard full of weeds? One weed at a time. And that's exactly what I did. Before I knew it, I looked around and it was done.

The path to true happiness can be like looking at a front

yard full of weeds. Our "one at a time" is one inspiring moment at a time. We compound our inspired experiences and, before we know it, we've been living inspired lives. We look around and realize we're truly happy. We're fulfilled. We're connected to your true selves.

Don't bother worrying about the yard of weeds. It will take the same amount of effort to complete if we worry about it for weeks or months or if we don't worry at all. In fact, worrying will probably delay us from action and allow *the voice* to confuse or even talk us out of it.

ALL BY MYSELF – THAT'S NOT SO BAD

It turns out I like weeding. I'm connected with nature, I'm outside, I can see my progress, I get some physical activity, I get to spend some time with myself, and sometimes I even put on Spanish lessons.

Though I realize I'll have to re-weed this same yard who knows how many times, I also know it has to be done now—and that's okay. I wouldn't claim that weeding inspires me, but I would say that threads of the experience tap into inspiration.

Weeding offers a measurable (visual) reward. I have to stop the normal grind of life, which allows some time to connect to myself. I can listen to nature, music or learn Spanish. I can be outside, and I love being outside. For me, this dreaded chore is not so bad. We can choose to find the inspirational threads if we seek to discover them.

CELEBRATE EACH INSPIRED MOMENT

Imagine your life if you celebrated each inspired moment, fully indulging in the present. The good times will feel more lasting, your life will feel fuller, and your feelings of happiness prolonged. Colors will be bolder. Flavors will offer deep trails of delight with every bite. That metaphorical rose you stopped to smell will fill your soul with enlivening fragrance.

What do you love to do? How can you take an extra

moment or even five minutes to celebrate? Ideally, we want to celebrate inspiration many times a day, but for now, you may be identifying with inspiration once a day or once a week. Pause long enough to let inspiration fill and recharge your entire body, mind and soul. Find the inspirational threads in everything and watch your usual day-to-day transform into the most magical, enjoyable and fulfilling life you could ever imagine.

STEP 4:

Apply Inspiration to Every Part of Your Life

"Plant your own garden and decorate your own soul, instead of waiting for someone to bring you flowers."

—Veronica Shoffstall

CHAPTER NINE

Get Inspired by Yourself

Since the caveman days, fear has been a powerful motivator that can influence our decision-making. Nowadays, however, we aren't running from wild animals, but instead are afraid of emotional trauma, change, disappointment and rejection. That voice of *what ifs* can smash our dreams in a matter of seconds (or days or years, depending on how long we let *the voice* interfere with our true desires).

Is part of you gnawing to go hang gliding? Cue the *what ifs* to hear all the reasons not to. Want to start your own business? *What ifs* run rampant!

While strategic thinking can certainly be important in decision-making, it helps to identify the requests that truly come from the depth of our true selves. These are the requests that don't need *the voice's* fearful and discouraging questions. These requests deserve to hear, "how can I make this happen?"

Sometimes our heart desires something that actually isn't

in alignment with our true selves. Our hearts might fear change, unpredictability or being alone. We are afraid of taking a temporary loss in happiness, love or security to restart on a new path to true happiness, true love and genuine emotional security. It often calls upon great courage, but sometimes we have to take a temporary setback in our happiness to invest in energy towards true happiness.

TUNE INTO YOUR TRUE SELF

I can acutely feel when something is calling me, even if my brain and heart are both resistant. Running definitely called me, and I really thought I hated running. If we learn to tune into our true selves, we start to hear our true needs a little louder, and that other *voice* becomes less important.

The great part about listening to our true selves is that it can give us courage to do things on our own. Want to get into cycling but don't have any friends that cycle (yet)? Do it on your own. Really want to see a movie that's out but you just moved to a new town and don't know anyone? Go by yourself! Want to go on a hike, but your partner doesn't want to go? Hike solo!

Sometimes the hardest part is doing the things that you want to alone, taking that first step when you really just wish *anyone* was with you. Maybe it would be more fun, but the journeys we take by ourselves, whether small or large, always have meaning and purpose. And after you do those things, you get the satisfaction of knowing you can indeed do it on your own—and be okay!

Don't wait for life to grab you and make you inspired. Take action to create your inspired life. Take control of your life, your choices, your actions, and lean into inspiration. That's how we attract friends and partners who enjoy the same things we do. Don't wait for someone *else* to inspire you or to drag you along on their inspirational path. Create your own path and your own unique, inspired and happy life, and then delight others with an invitation to share alongside.

If you are waiting for someone or something, choose to stop waiting. Do something on your own; something you've been avoiding or denying because you'd rather do it with someone else. Make a choice to change your mentality today and take action. You are the only person holding you back from your inspired life, and you can inspire yourself!

OUR SECRET INSPIRED WORLD

There is a secret world only able to be discovered by those who know about it—a world of beauty, magical moments, and inspired experiences at every turn. How do we find this world?

I was visiting friends, and set out on a walk in the early evening while the sun was still up. We were talking and enjoying each other's company. We stepped through the final gate and my friends proceeded down the stairs to the sidewalk. I, however, was transported to a magical place.

The stairs were decorated in gorgeous purple flower petals. Bright, bold, delicate and colorful, paving the way forward. I looked up to see what I now know are tibouchina urvilleana, or princess flower trees, alive with a stunning color pop of my favorite shade of purple. Their delicacy was disproportionate to their bold colors and outstretched pollen tentacles. I stopped in awe of this magical place.

In the middle of concrete surroundings, across the street from a Target, I was fully present in an inspired moment. And it was just for me. I probably looked silly to my companions. I was so lost and found in this gift. I was in my own secret inspired world, and I stopped and spent a couple minutes to fill my soul with this inspired moment.

It was okay that I was in my secret inspired world by myself because inspiration is subjective. In this case, it was my favorite color in my favorite shade, guiding me down a path and encompassing me in every direction. Intensified by the element of surprise, this discovery inspired me, and it's okay that it didn't mean as much to anyone else I was with. Part of what makes inspired moments so special is that they are personal.

Inspired moments are everywhere, regardless if we see them, seek them or are in a space to take them in or not. We can find delight and surprise in the most mundane circumstances and the most generic of spaces. Allowing ourselves to indulge in these magical surprise moments provides a powerful recharge. I could have been embarrassed by how much this beauty inspired me, quickly dismissing it and walking down the stairs to fit in or seem "normal." But for what purpose? I would rather let these moments and experiences fill my soul.

Sometimes they are once in a lifetime, and we don't have to feel silly pausing to appreciate the unique specialness of what inspires us. If we lose ourselves fully in the enjoyment of an inspired moment, being intensely present and filled with inspiration, we'll collect reference points that run deep to our true selves. When we make a deep connection with life, we create a chord to easily access and re-experience our most inspired moments again and again.

You may be familiar with the "double rainbow" reaction video, popular on YouTube. If you haven't seen it, consider it homework and search "double rainbow" by Yosemitebear62. The man with the camera, one-time MMA fighter Paul "Bear" Vasquez, is caught by complete surprise in an inspired moment. He literally doesn't know what to do with himself. Even though he is filming the moment, he's not at all thinking of what he *should* be saying or doing.

While it's funny because of his dramatic reaction, to put it lightly, this man lost himself completely in inspiration. While some may say, "that's beautiful," take a photo and move on, for him, it was just the right phenomenon at just the right time.

The experience of seeing the majestic double rainbow transported him to his secret inspired world. Fully present, with no regard for anyone else's judgment, forgetting any "to do" list or that anything else even mattered—he was in that magical space.

While I admittedly laughed throughout this video, I also felt uncomfortable. I think because I felt like I was infringing on his secret inspired world. This was *his* inspired moment. His experience is just so pure. He is so free. It's raw, unedited, unadulterated emotion. You don't have to film it or share it with the world, or even be so vocal about it, but we could all be so lucky to find and lose ourselves in inspired moments to this degree in our internal experience.

Need an escape from all the stress, pressures and baggage we may hold onto? You could have a drink or you could lose yourself in an inspired moment. "Losing yourself" is completely ironic, because in these moments, you are the most in tune with your true self. You are the most "found" a person, soul or spirit can be.

*"Eating good food is about respecting your body
as much as it is about delighting your palate
with intricate flavors and textures."[1]*

—Brigitte Thériault

CHAPTER TEN

Get Inspired in Your Body

We know if we are inspired in our bodies. We know if we feel good about the physical choices we are making. We know if we supporting our bodies to have energy, mobility and endurance.

Self-care is a major thread of inspiration that is woven into being inspired in our bodies. While many of us would have to work really hard to be inspired *by* our bodies, those of us who don't want to work that hard still have a responsibility to be in alignment with our true selves. Taking care of our bodies is an important part of living the inspired life.

Our bodies are our vehicles of life. They are ours to take care of. If we aren't taking care of them, they show signs of stress and wear. If we are taking care of our bodies, they show signs of healing and resiliency. A healthy body is an inspired body, and an inspired body is a happy body.

If we are not inspired to take care of our bodies, inspired

by eating healthily and some form of being active, we place limitations, or a ceiling, on how far inspiration can take us in our capacity to be happy.

Being inspired in our bodies is not foundationally about loving our bodies or being thin. If we're dreaming about a perfect body or obsessing about what we don't like about our bodies, we're pursuing the wrong focus. We don't need to focus on what we don't like about our bodies in order to be motivated to change. Our bodies mostly reflect how connected we are to our true selves, so you can skip self-criticism and jump straight to focusing on honoring your true self through honoring your body.

There are many physical ailments that can prevent us from having the body we want or having as active a body as we'd like. Those with disabilities, or temporary or permanent physical ailments that reduce their ability to participate in all the inspiring activities they'd like, are being called upon to have courage every day and are an inspiration to those around them. If the focus is on being inspired rather than physical limitations, we can feed our souls, spirits, and inspire our bodies to be as healthy and strong as they can be, regardless of any limits on our physical abilities.

Even when we're making inspired choices, our bodies will not change in a day, so we must give ourselves a break from judging what we don't like about ourselves physically.

Let's not focus on how our bodies look, but focus on how our bodies feel. Do your best to help your body feel inspired every day. If you are in alignment with your true self and focusing on what inspires you and your body, your body has its best chance to be healthier and happier by default as a direct result of your choices.

We must not take our bodies or our health for granted. Especially as we age, we will face physical setbacks at some point, but we can build a strong immune system by eating healthily and getting regular exercise. We can remain committed to doing the best we can to fuel our body with what inspires it: healthy fuel and activity.

Let's celebrate our healthiest times by maximizing our inspired activities that someday we may not be able to do as easily. Fuel your body to maximize your energy, mobility and endurance, and you'll be able to do more of what inspires you and feel great doing it.

WHY WE DON'T TAKE CARE OF OUR BODIES

We don't always eat healthily or exercise because we simply don't want to. Sometimes junk food tastes better. It's cheaper and easier. "I'm tired. I need to veg out. I'm too tired to cook. It's too cold/hot to go outside. I don't want to pay for a gym/yoga/etc. membership. I don't want it that badly (until I get depressed about it most other moments)."

A lot of diets don't work because they are about *"I'll be happy when."* They are based on control. They feel oppressive.

Now's the time to focus on the *why* of our goals and not the *what.* Our *why's* for dieting or eating healthy might include having more energy to spend with our family, having more strength and endurance playing our favorite sport, experiencing less injuries, ailments or sicknesses, having less pain in our bodies, being more physically capable to do more of what inspires us, and so on.

If we only focus on how many pounds we want to lose or what we don't like about our bodies, we'll miss the magic of the journey. Enjoy feeling good being active and eating well because it inspires you, not because you can see changes each time. If we can't find a way to tap into inspiration, we either won't be successful in our goals or we will be miserable while we're on the journey.

One of the tenets of Alcoholic's Anonymous is "one day at a time." How about one meal at a time? It's like my relationship with weeding. We don't want to do it. We don't know how long it will take. The feat ahead is too overwhelming. It's not what we *want* to do.

This pushback indicates you're disconnected from your true self. Picture a kid crying and screaming, "I don't want to!" If that kid sometimes makes appearances inside of you, rest assured you can calm him or her by letting your adult true self take over.

Such protests are common in far more than just body-related work. Tasks at your job that you really don't want to do? Put them off! The relationship you know isn't good for you anymore, but you still love him/her? Stay together!

That's the child or the heart or the addiction or the cravings blocking your true self. Since all that work is out of the scope of these pages, let's focus on what we can do right now.

We need to find a thread of inspiration we can apply to our bodies and health. Don't like running? A gym membership is too expensive? Don't want to be embarrassed in front of the cross-fit pros? Then don't do those things. Stop using all those excuses and create an inspired solution: Do a YouTube yoga video for free in your living room.

I never liked Brussels sprouts, until I found a recipe for roasting them with just some olive oil, garlic, salt and pepper. The classic Brussels sprout didn't change, I just changed the way I approached it. It was so simple, and yet transformed something I proclaimed I didn't like into something I enjoy.

We are capable of changing our enjoyment of activities and life in general. A friend lost 80 pounds by turning to clean eating and exercise. She had to learn how to cook. She had to learn how to exercise. She had to get over the self-consciousness of being in the "men's" section of the gym. And now she is a wealth of knowledge and talks about being a coach one day for other women who started where she did.

We don't need to go to an extreme, but we do need to find at least one physical activity, even if it's just a casual stroll in the great outdoors, and one healthy meal a day that we can get inspired about. Once we spark that inspiration, it will catch fire and light up other inspirating opportunities and choices.

THE INSPIRATION-ONLY DIET

I love ice cream. As I noted earlier, sometimes I eat ice cream to "make me happy," which really doesn't make me happy in the end because I could eat until my stomach hurts and still not be happy.

I can also eat ice cream because it inspires me. When I was traveling throughout Italy, I tried different gelato flavors everywhere we went, savoring each and every inspiring bite. I enjoyed each delicious moment, not knowing if I would ever have this same gelato again. I was fulfilled, energized, grateful and inspired.

Inspiring our bodies doesn't have to mean eating measured amounts of chicken and veggies every night. You can enjoy the flavors and creativity of food. What if you went on an inspiration-only diet? What if the natural outcome of eating from an internally inspired space was to eat smaller quantities of the less healthy foods that inspire us and not eat those we eat mindlessly?

We know when we're eating because we're bored, because we think it will make us happy (when no amount is enough), and when we're so inspired by the moment that our consumption is slow, present and fulfilling.

If we only eat from an inspired place, we'll likely eat less because we'll be eating slowly and be more fulfilled physically and emotionally. We won't need to binge or eat junk all day, and we'll be more motivated to give our body the healthy fuel it needs because we also get to enjoy the food that inspires us in fulfilling moderation.

Food ads often show someone slowly, carefully biting into a delightful morsel. Maybe the cheese lingers as it stretches towards the mouth or the spoon lingers too long on the lips longer, accentuating how much the consumer is enjoying whatever they are selling. Eyes open a little wider in pleasant surprise, nodding "yes, so good," or smiling with such bliss during and after the bite.

What if you could be that delighted with every bite? Make those indulgent moments, whether savory or sweet, so fulfilling that they are inspiring enough to be taken in reasonable portions.

EXERCISING MAKES INSPIRED EATING EASIER

Beyond the obvious benefits of exercise for physical health, I shared how exercise helps me eat better throughout the day. As if the benefits of keeping my body active, strong, and recharged weren't compelling enough, exercise also allows me to burn some calories, start my workday having already made time for myself, and it motivates me to not waste that effort. My willpower is infinitely more powerful after I exercise in the morning. Not only am I less tempted by goodies in the break room, but I also want to eat healthier foods to make the most of the sleep I sacrificed the effort I made in the morning.

I was surprised to learn that walking may burn fat more effectively than running. My friend who lost 80 pounds and is now an official gym rat said she lost the most weight when she was doing two 45 minute walks a day.

Interval training can also be effective. I did a lot of research on heart rate training, purchased a wrist heart rate monitor that didn't work then got a real heart rate monitor with a chest strap, and now can time my intervals and their intensity to exactly what is effective for my body. In 30 minutes on my treadmill at home, I can get a great, effective workout.

While it's important that I mix up my treadmill "routines," interval training is said to continue burning fat throughout the day even after your workout.[2] My routines include 45 minute outdoor walks, 30-45 minute incline walks, intervals walk/runs at intensities of 65% and 90%, and, every now and then, a jog for my heart health. I was surprised to discover that even jogging could shoot my heart rate into my anaerobic zone for heart health rather than the typical aerobic zone for weight loss.

I CAN'T RUN

I can't begin to count the many times I've told the story of why I learned to hate running. And here I go again. When I was 13, I was in a junior lifeguards summer program. I always finished among the last three people in runs or run-swim-runs. The frustration and humiliation led me to claim that I was terrible at running and I hated it. Telling that story so many times perpetuated my defeat, frustration and humiliation, but I didn't know what else to do. I didn't know what was "wrong" with me.

Years later, while doing some research on heart rates, I learned why my experiences with running were so terrible. My heart rate shoots up into uncomfortable levels when I run, quickly making it difficult to breathe and making my chest hurt. I also have a small gait, meaning I have to move my legs faster to keep up with someone who has a larger gait. Between trying to keep up and having my heart rate so high, I was working too hard![3]

When exercising in heart rate zones that are too high, you are exerting more energy than needed for effective weight loss or anaerobic training, therefore increasing your risk of injury[4] without reward.

For two decades, I told myself and others that I can't run! But, in reality, if I run slowly and don't compare myself to others who run with ease, I don't hate running. It becomes doable for me, and that's what's most important. Breaking the defeat, frustration and humiliation that I've reinforced each time I've said, "I can't run and I hate running!" inspires me to believe that I am capable of changing, even after twenty years.

FOCUS ON THE INSPIRED *WHY*, NOT THE *WHAT*

Connect with the *why's* that inspire your body. Do you

101

want to have more energy to run around with your kids? Do you want to unlock opportunities to travel more? Do you want to experience less pain in your body? Do you want to prolong your life to ensure your bucket list is checked off? Do you feel more confident when you take care of yourself, helping you participate in all the activities you enjoy without limitations?

Make a list or inspirational photo board of the *why's*. Don't obsess as much about *what's*. Make a list or use photos to remind you *why* you're inspired to make choices that honor and inspire your body.

THE BODY ALWAYS KNOWS

The amount of stress our body is capable of holding is ridiculous. We may not even know what we are capable of carrying until we are sore, in pain, sick, having a "flare up," or diagnosed with a disease. While I do not believe that every pain or disease is from unresolved stress, I do believe that stress is the number one cause of physical ailments directly or indirectly.

Our body will carry an exorbitant amount of stress, harming our immune system without us even knowing. When we hold on to anger or bury resentment, we can carry that negative energy physically for decades. It has to live somewhere, and the longer we carry it and the further we bury it, the deeper it goes into our body. It stores in fat, muscles, and bones.

Louise Hay has done some interesting research that indicates how specific causes of stress can show up physically in specific ways. If this interests you, check out her book, *You Can Heal Your Life*.[5]

We know stressing about being stressed doesn't help, but it's not always easy to simply shake it off. The more we need our body to get healthier, the more stressed we get if we can't make it happen immediately. Even acne can result from stress, but how do you stop stressing when you're seeing proof of your stress every time you look in a mirror?

Instead of focusing on the stress, especially since we know thought suppression doesn't work, replace that focus with getting inspired. If you can't easily change what is stressing you, start collecting inspired moments to change your experience of each day.

If you are still holding on to stress or worrying about what has happened in the past, remember that you are in complete control of how you experience the future.

*"The whales do not sing because they have an answer,
they sing because they have a song."*

—Gregory Colbert

CHAPTER ELEVEN

Shared Inspiration

Inspiration is magnetic. Since inspiration is authentic by default, it immediately attracts an authentic reaction, curiosity, and passion in others who share the same inspiration. Connecting through inspiration is powerful, empowering and strengthening. It doesn't matter what the inspiration is. When you get to "geek out" with people "just like you," the combination of self-expression and shared acceptance is healing.

There are so many ways to share inspiration today, whether in person or online. Connect with others through existing channels or make your own! Join or create a meet-up group, team or club. Blog in an online community. Use ub:inspired to connect with those who have shared inspiration, goal and bucket list items.

We have all experienced the energy in a venue filled with shared inspiration—concerts, sporting events, churches, marathons, the unveiling of a new innovative product, a lab when a cure is discovered, and so on. The intensity is tangible. When shared by group, the experience of excitement, focus and being present is amplified. Emotions are high; we are vulnerable, yet strong. We are free.

One person is enough to inspire the world. One quote can quench the souls of millions. One voice can start a revolution.

One dream can tap into the dreams of many, naturally strengthened as it grows to inspire an ever-increasing number of people.

When we are shining in our inspiration, those around us shine, too. When someone sees us in an inspired moment, they can't help but to light up with inspiration themselves. Being inspired is so pure that it is contagious in the best of ways. It doesn't matter if you're watching an amazing athlete score, a child who loves to sing, or a professor who cares so deeply about a subject that he or she lights up naturally—that inspired light makes us want to have and share our own inspired light, even if we aren't a star athlete, can't hold a tune, or don't know anything about the professor's preferred subject of delight.

When we are truly passionate about a cause, it is always personal. When our passion for a cause comes from an inspired place, it naturally invites others to share in the inspired moment, for that cause or even another. Since inspiration is immune to rejection and adversity, it doesn't matter how many followers join our cause and share in our inspiration. That is always secondary and, in the end, irrelevant. Equal rights causes have taken years or decades or lifetimes to be realized. While social change may be a goal in causes for which we advocate, expressing our truths in the present always comes first.

When we try to make other people do what we want them to, we can become frustrated if they don't comply in a short time frame—or ever. But when we are inspired, simply being inspired is enough, and we certainly won't stop, quit or become frustrated if others aren't as inspired as we are about a given cause, activity or topic. It may be disappointing if others don't share in our inspiration, but we don't give up because it's really about being true to and expressing ourselves. Adversity never puts out our inspired light!

"Too many irons, not enough fire."

—S. Kelley Harrell

CHAPTER TWELVE

Get Inspired at Work

Please count how many times the words "stress" and "inspired" are used in the following definition of "work," courtesy of Merriam-Webster[1]:

1: activity in which one exerts strength or faculties to do or perform something:
    a : sustained physical or mental effort to overcome obstacles and achieve an objective or result
    b : the labor, task, or duty that is one's accustomed means of livelihood
    c : a specific task, duty, function, or assignment often being a part or phase of some larger activity

I counted zero for both words. It seems we can choose whether we want work to be stressful or if we want work to be inspired. Neither is required.

If our job is a prevailing source of stress, feeling oppressed (to burden spiritually or mentally; weigh heavily upon) and generally uninspired, we have to either change our mindset or our job. Maybe even our career.

Our work, where we spend at least half of our waking hours, should be in close alignment with something that inspires us. We have the *most* choice about where we work and what we do, and we have a decent amount of control over how to get there.

We can go to school, select a field of study, and choose how hard we work to get grades (or, better yet, to be present and retain what we learn and understand how to apply it).

We can learn outside of school, with an entrepreneurial spirit, finding real world opportunities to provide the experience we need. We can get internships, find mentors, or learn online with the plethora of digital resources and programs at our fingertips.

We have more ways than ever before to pursue the job or career path that inspires us, and none are without challenges. It will take time and commitment, as there are few shortcuts to learning and practicing, but we experience the reward for the rest of our lives.

Most importantly, we can start a journey to a new job or career any time. It's one thing if our job simply isn't working for us, but if our career is creating a ceiling of happiness, it is never too late to prepare for another field.

Maybe you need to take a pay cut. Maybe you need four years of school or an advanced degree. As daunting as these options are, one year in a job that inspires you will quickly wash away the time spent to get there.

To live the inspired life, some of us will need to feel inspired in our jobs, but some of us can feel neutral in our day jobs and live the inspired life outside of work, still tapping into true happiness.

I know folks that show up, do their job, and enjoy an inspired life as soon as they clock out. While perhaps not achieving the greatest inspiration possible, these folks are likely happier than those taking their uninspired-ness home or feeling oppressed by their work. It's important to honor this difference in experience. This chapter is primarily aimed at those who feel their job might be a drain on their life rather than a tool or positive energy source to live the inspired life.

THAT STORY AGAIN: WHAT WE SAY MATTERS

Pay attention to how you talk about your job to others. What do you say? If you say something like "eh, it's alright" or even "I hate it" for an extended period of time, why would you settle for that? Money? Predictability? There are many circumstances in which these needs are quite real, like having a big mortgage, paying off debt, or financially supporting others. But there may be ways to fulfill those obligations other than sacrificing your ability to live a happy life by staying in a long-term job that doesn't inspire you.

If we must fulfill other responsibilities, at least for now, rather than pursuing a job that truly inspires, then our only choice is to change our attitude. We can bet if we don't like our jobs, we're not the only one who knows it. We can become a drain on our co-workers, bosses and even customers or clients.

Identify a fulfilling part of your job and work to enhance it. Do it more, do it even better, or get training. Look at promotion opportunities or discover what new tasks or roles you can take to change it up a bit.

Is there a small or large change you can make in your current job that would make a big difference for you? Ask for what you want. So many opportunities are left on the table because we try to predict an answer based on assumptions. Advocate for yourself if no one else is advocating for you.

For those who aren't under tangible duress to stay in a job, besides the excuses that will likely flow regardless, one great way to change it up is to enhance your knowledge or skills by learning something new. Whether you learn on your own time or request paid training, learning sparks excitement and fulfillment as we break out of the same old patterns and are able to contribute more than before.

In the end, if our working environment is unhealthy, no amount of inspiration or mindset will break through that ceiling. If we are not being treated with respect or are being subjected to negativity or ridicule day after day, it will eventually eat away at our self-esteem or possibly cause us to develop habitual defense mechanisms that may be inappropriate and unnecessary at our next workplace. We might forget that a work environment can be healthy and enjoyable, and the longer we stay in dysfunction, the more likely we will darkly color any job, or even the world, as an unsafe or offensive place that doesn't truly see us or our worth.

We simply deserve better, and the longer we allow ourselves to be subjected to unhealthy behavior, the lower our ceiling of happiness (and self worth).

WHAT'S STOPPING YOU FROM YOUR DREAM JOB

I'm not talking about running a sunscreen sales hut on a beach in Hawaii. This might be a "dream job," but it's generally based on escape, not inspiration. It might be short lived, you might get bored, or you might just need a vacation. So, let's restate the question: What is your dream job that is fueled by inspiration?

If we really explore what we love to do, we can start to see ways to make money doing it. Maybe not as much money as we'd like, but enough, coupled with the fulfillment of living your inspiration every day to compensate.

Think about someone who has your dream job. What did they do differently to get to that spot? Outside of literal physical circumstances, there is likely nothing to stop you from taking the same path except your own fear and self doubt. Didn't they take the same risks you're afraid to take?

The book, *The Four Hour Work Week* by Tim Ferris[2], is not based on doing what inspires us for money. Rather it is focused on how to work less to have more time for enjoying and living the inspired life. While some of his most extreme principles may be difficult for many to adopt, it still is an inspiring look at what's possible and it provides a refresh on how free we can be from traditional views, expectations and excuses around our standard jobs. This book inspired me to think outside the box I'd come to accept around what work "had" to be.

Summarizing what we've discovered so far, if we want to live the inspired life, we have two options regarding our relationship with work: 1) work in a job that doesn't inspire us so we can afford what does, or 2) work in a job that inspires us on a foundational level.

The idea of quitting to work an inspired job can be terrifying, but if we talk with or read blogs from those who have, we'll find their writing is hardly gloomy or filled with fear. It's alive with inspiration! It's energizing and motivating to read. While some realities and responsibilities may settle in, we can find a way to make money from inspiring activities. Not only will you be better than most at what inspires you, but your passion will be contagious, infused in your work, inspiring your customers and providing infinite opportunities for soul-quenching and monetary rewards.

WHEN WE HAVE TO CHANGE MORE THAN OUR MINDSET

Sometimes inspiration isn't enough to make our jobs work. Sometimes we get tired of keeping our heads bent under a happiness ceiling that is simply too low for us.

I went through a period of having a tough time at work. I was unhappy too often. To compensate, I started wearing bolder and brighter colors because color inspires me. I began putting positive quotes in front of my computer monitor. I bought a $45 magic healing scent oil to put behind my ears. I was really, *really* trying to change the experience of my day. In the end, what I needed was to change my job. Sometimes it is just time.

Inspiration is only a temporary fix if we are unable to influence our environment, or the people and circumstances within it, to get what we need. Inspiration isn't enough to change an unhealthy work or home environment into a healthier one. Inspiration is not enough to give you everything you need to be truly happy if we continue to keep fundamental parts of our lives out of alignment with our true selves.

Sometimes these situations are temporary, and we must stay strong to get to a bigger reward or fulfillment on the other side. Other times, we are simply enduring stress and trying our best to ignore what our true selves need because we think we "should," have to, or are uncomfortable with the unknown that will follow a departure from an existing job or career.

I enjoyed that job for years, but it was time for a transition. My next position represented a substantial cut in combined pay and benefits. Prior to leaving, I experienced a clear realization that my happiness shouldn't be held hostage by money. By staying, I was trading fulfillment for what I considered significant money. I had been selling my happiness, and it finally stopped being okay. I sought a more inspiring work environment with reduced stress and enjoyed my life more, even with the financial hit. I've never regretted it.

And now I'm taking the far greater risk of quitting my job to go backpacking in South America for three months, returning home to build my own business doing the work I love the most: creating inspiring messaging and content to benefit business and organizations through branding and marketing.

I have been inspired by brand building since I was a kid. I've always said that I didn't choose marketing, marketing chose me. I want to do the highest concentration of the work I love the most. I will be coming home from our trip without a job lined up, but I'll return focused on doing what inspires me and trusting that my best chance of success will come by starting with my true self. Regardless, the financial implications and risks of what I'm about to do make any previous worry over my pay cut ridiculously laughable.

When we know what our souls need, it becomes too loud to ignore. I realized that I have to dive in and give it all I have. I will be okay if I'm doing what inspires me. I can't go wrong if I'm starting from the source of inspiration. I can't be broke forever. I can always be an uber driver, have roommates, couchsurf, or do whatever is needed to pursue my dream job and my dream life. I am the only person holding me back. Not only is life too short to not live the inspired life, it is too long to spend it uninspired.

WHAT IF YOUR PATH WAS AS WIDE AS THE WORLD?

Pam is a successful businesswoman by all standards. She is a partner of a well-established, highly respected local insurance company. She is poised, professional and grounded. She also works on a rainwater catchment program in remote Amazon villages in South America to provide safe drinking water.

She stays in lightly sheltered cots in the middle of the jungle, dumping out her shoes each morning to make sure a variety of over-sized insects haven't found a new home where her toes belong. She spends time in villages where there are no toilets, doctors or stores. She continues to go back, even after an extremely dangerous experience when a storm hit their boat on the Amazon River.

You might assume she is tapping into the energy of her early 30's, but that's not the case. With three grandkids and one Peruvian godchild, Pam is fueled by inspiration!

"My real passion is education, and I wanted to provide educational materials to children in these remote areas. But I learned that one in five children under five are dying from contaminated water. On my first trip, I saw children who were sick, and I knew I had to do something."

She connected with two NGO's and currently works with Engineers Without Borders Sonoma to develop rainwater containment systems in these villages. Her team completed their first project in 2005. She is a project facilitator and fund-raiser. As of 2015, there are seven completed projects, with two more to be finished within six months.

In 2003, she started helping a micro business of alpaca weavers, which was a dream of hers. She established an import company, selling the products in the USA and using the profits to help fund the water project.

When I asked Pam about how it feels to be so far out of her comfort zone in those remote Amazonian Villages, she lights up and responds, "but I'm not out of my comfort zone. I'm in my element! When I'm there, I know there will be new challenges and unknowns, but my response is, 'bring it on!' I just feel so happy when I'm there." Pam is energized, empowered and definitely inspired!

At first glance, it seems like two different people living in two different worlds—a strategic business woman by day and an Amazon explorer, philanthropist and volunteer by night! But for Pam, all of these experiences create a balanced and full inspired life.

We don't have to be at work all the time and we don't have to be living in the Amazon all the time, and, above all, we don't have to identify with one or another. Pam is inspired by doing well in her business, traveling, being outdoors and helping others, and she's found creative and impactful ways to combine these.

"I spent a lot of time outdoors as a kid. I saw how my father remained calm when we had a run in with a bear and when a small plane we were on had to make a dangerous emergency landing. I remember being scared, but I saw that we got through it. I've been in many dangerous situations, but I never let the fear of what might happen stop me from fully living my life."

Pam goes on one big trip every other year, exploring the world's most inspiring cities, historical sights and cultural experiences. She enjoys delightful culinary experiences, local theater performances, world-wide adventures, and spending time connecting with her community. In between, she works on her Amazonian water projects and spends time sharing her passion for life with her grandkids.

Pam proves that you don't have to choose one lifestyle over another. Life is full of inspired moments, experiences and adventures that she compounds together to live her happiest life.[3]

WHEN QUITTERS PROSPER

Jessica spent four years in law school, incurring a large student loan debt in the process, and then spent more money to prepare for the bar exam. Initially inspired by the promised security of a well-paying, stable job in the legal field, why would she, at age 47, even imagine changing careers?

After ultimately choosing not to go into practice as a lawyer, hoping instead to find another legal career path, she tried on various professional hats. During this time, she also experienced an emotionally turbulent relationship that led her to the Al-anon community and into therapy. And so began a journey of soul searching and finally shedding layer after layer of dysfunctional blockages that kept her true self buried.

As her journey continued, she discovered that she was inspired by so much in the world, and yet she wasn't living her life to its inspired potential. She was sacrificing inspiration in exchange for ensuring her security and justifying her time and financial investment in her legal career.

As she dug deeper, she began to see a parallel evident in the quality of her romantic and personal relationships and her daily work environment. She realized that, despite feeling like she was showing up and offering her best in those contexts, her professional efforts and her playful and creative personality were not valued, reciprocated or even fully welcomed. While being self-supporting was a goal and something she would be proud of, she saw that, for her, it came at too high a cost—increased stress, a very long commute, and ultimately, tremendous regret about choosing the path to a legal career.

She remembers a moment where she "began to imagine her life differently." It came finally after identifying and accepting the many uninspiring qualities of her life and the detrimental impact they were having on her well-being. In meditation and times of self-reflection, she found some form of guidance through accepting what wasn't working and, moreover, her part in all of it. By not fully valuing her inner or true self that was meant to live un-beholden to the wants and criticisms of others, she had not created positive boundaries in relationships. Self-worth and healthy boundaries emerged as new concepts and opportunities.

Jessica began to write a well-being list about what she wanted for her life, specifically listing the qualities inherent in the experiences she deeply believed represented her well-being. These included feeling welcomed and appreciated by the people she interacted with at work, in her family, and in platonic friendships; not commuting; being able to bring her dog to work (why not?!); a healthy romantic relationship; starting a family; and living a healthy lifestyle. She also included a long time passion—making art, and the initial goal that prompted the pursuit of a legal career—to help people.

During the following months, she actively searched for better employment opportunities and focused on a daily gratitude practice. Workplace stress continued to increase, as did the fear of losing her job and thus her ability to be self-supporting. After one very negative experience at work, she sat staring at her well-being checklist and wondered if maybe she should streamline it and add some sense of urgency. "Yoga, beaches, music, dancing, art—NOW!"

Jessica is a very creative person. In fact, "creating" itself is a major source of inspiration for her, as it is for many. She wanted to feel inspired again, and for more than the too-few moments that came while making art or hiking.

There came a point when she knew she simply had to turn off *the voice* of fear and anxiety and let inspiration guide her.

Today, the list of qualities on her well-being list is how she describes her life. At age 48, she has happily left her legal career to work at a nonprofit that welcomes her authenticity, provides the flexibility for self-care when she needs it, and serves as an outlet to recharge with inspiration.

Once the unsatisfying and stressful job was behind her, she focused on making more art, new friends, and seeking inspiration in everyday life. As she became more comfortable just being her true self, the quality of her experiences and relationships shifted, doors opened while others closed, and a new path was revealed. She's taking what inspires her and is infusing it into her new career, even creating a pottery-focused fundraiser.

When she looks back and sees how dramatically every aspect of her life has changed, she feels gratitude, which fuels more inspiration. The "how-to" wasn't easy, but it was simple. She had to do some intense personal work to let go of the years and dollars spent on creating a sure path in the legal world. Sometimes choosing to live the inspired life isn't the most convenient, secure or financially compelling, but it is infinitely rich in soul-quenching rewards.

During that year of transition, she focused on creating a body of functional pottery to sell. Her mantra that year had been "InJoy," and it appeared on most of her pieces. When people asked for the meaning, she simply said, "it's a reminder for me to do the things big and small that cause a feeling of joy, and that I can live InJoy every day when I do."[4]

๛

As I am weeks away from quitting my job to kick-off a new inspiring chapter in my life, I can reflect on how "not me" this decision would have been during the first thirty years of my life. I would never take a risk of the unknown, would never use a line of credit to fund anything that I wasn't certain would be paid back that month, and would never quit a job without something lined up for the next day. I'm so glad my "never's" turned out to be just temporary labels and limitations I put on my potential.

I don't use the word "never" anymore. I've seen too much change to ever think I can predict how I'll feel or what I'll want at a given time. My true self is the foundation of who I am, but this journey is over the course of my lifetime, and I continue to shed layers to further uncover my true self. Who knows what I'll want or how I'll feel after I return from months of showerless days, sleeping without my Tempurpedic mattress and challenging myself to be okay outside of the comforts of my daily life. I don't have to know how I'll feel *then* in order to move forward *now*, but I trust that if I lead with inspiration, opportunities will unfold.

It's never too late to change your job or your career in the spirit of seeking inspiration. There are a lot of reasons why it won't be convenient or feel secure or be financially compelling, but if we focus instead on how we can infuse inspiration into a job or career, we can focus on finding ways to make it possible.

"The power of getting to know one another is so immense, eclipsed only by first getting to know ourselves."

—Bryant McGill

CHAPTER THIRTEEN

Get Inspired in Relationships

INSPIRATION IN DATING

If you're in the dating world, consider focusing the over-used "get to know them questions" to discover what inspires your date! This line of discovery is the quickest way to determine compatibility. We can unveil a whole new side of our date when they talk about what inspires them rather than their favorite movie.

First, a quick note on finding "the one." It's *easy* to fall in love. Two single people looking for that special something in someone else, getting lost in the ideas and promises of a perfect life together, mixed with chemistry and attraction—it's easy to fall in love with a person's great qualities.

But it's the rest of the stuff that matters for a long-term partnership. Sharing inspiration provides an opportunity to connect and re-connect, infusing positive energy into the relationship when things get too routine or tough.

While some dating websites might call this concept "shared interests," we know the energy around inspiration is so much more powerful than an uninspiring piece of paper with check-boxes on it.

There is an important difference between liking, tolerating, or participating in an activity and actually being inspired by the activity. Determining the difference is a clear way to get to inspired compatibility.

We all want a partner who will tolerate or join us in something we enjoy every now and then, like the classic sports game or symphony example where your partner entertains your inspired enjoyment of the experience as a gesture of love. But there are likely some inspired activities or beliefs in which you know you want to *share* in the inspiration, and we don't want a day-to-day life of our partner simply tolerating what's most important to our soul.

If hiking inspires you and you want to have hiking as an important part of your life, find someone who is also inspired by hiking. You will likely hike more if hiking also inspires your partner.

While it's certainly not required or needed for every aspect of your life, know which important activities inspire you that you want to share with a partner, and don't compromise. If you want to spend 30 years with someone, choose someone that is a partner in your life as fully as you desire.

It's also important to maintain inspiration that's just your own or that you share with others outside your relationship. You probably know deep down what inspiring experiences you want to share with a partner over the course of your lifetime, those that will help you live your life to the fullest. These may only represent a few from your inspiration list, and it's good to have plenty more that you'll be quite happy doing without a partner.

Compatibility is easy to overlook once emotions start flowing and we're struggling to figure out what we can settle for and what we can't. It's easier to let our hearts make the decisions at that point, but incompatibility will always surface eventually, whether it's about lifestyle, values or shared inspiration. The heart part is the easy part about love, so make the hard decisions about compatibility first and you'll be keeping room open for those that both share inspiration with you and can win your heart.

Use your inspiration list to choose which items you'd like to share with a partner. When you meet someone, gauge if they truly share some of your most desired shared inspiration items. Let's say your ideal partner is someone who is inspired by actively being in nature, enjoying great cuisine, and exploring the world. In this case, you don't need a second date with someone who doesn't like to hike, isn't a foodie, and really doesn't care to travel.

If you choose a partner that isn't inspired by what you know deep down you want to share, you likely won't participate in those activities as often as you would like, leading to a life less inspired than you may truly desire.

And here's a red flag hint: if you can't figure out at least three things that inspire a potential partner, move on. A healthy partner will know themselves (and not just mirror what you like), will have self worth and drive to pursue their passions, will not be waiting for the right person to get inspired or start living their lives, and will have that inspired energy ready to bring your relationship *up* without expecting you to do it for them.

If you continue dating without fundamental compatibility and shared inspiration being a prerequisite, you aren't leaving room for those that can genuinely provide it.

INSPIRATION IN RELATIONSHIPS

Those who have spent years in a relationship may struggle with how to stay connected and keep the love burning. It starts with being connected to our true selves, which creates our path to a happy and healthy life and relationship. We are able to share our best selves when we are living an inspired life.

By indulging in inspiration and keeping up on our inspiration, goal and bucket lists, we can show up as a happy, fulfilled and energetic partner with so much to offer.

The next step is to participate in or discover new inspiration together. There are infinite ways to discover inspiration, whether little moments, big trips, free experiences, and expensive activities.

Make an inspiration list as a couple. What inspired you when you first got together? What inspiration have you picked up along the way? If life is feeling too routine, find inspiring ways to not only stay connected together, but to fall in love with life all over again.

Most best practices with getting inspired ourselves are shared in creating happy and healthy relationships. Our relationship can only be as healthy as we are, and similarly, our relationship can only be as inspired as we are. Up the inspiration quotient to increase opportunities to connect. Try new things and be curious about what inspires your partner.

Emotional intimacy is most meaningful and profoundly felt when we share our true selves with our partner and when we create a loving space for our partner to do the same. Use inspiration to stay connected to yourself and your partner, and you'll experience the deepest joys and fulfillment a relationship has to offer.

WHEN IT'S NOT WORKING

Before we are in a serious, committed relationship, we can run rampant with our "bad" behavior. We can do what we want, say what we want and live how we want without having to consider the thoughts, feelings or preferences of a spouse or partner.

But once in a committed relationship, grappling with compromise and having a constant accountability mirror can be intense.

We have to work through behavior that isn't serving us as adults or isn't respectful or productive in our relationship.

If we're on the receiving end of behavior that doesn't feel loving or respectful, we can voice that we do not want to be subjected to the behavior. But if it persists and we don't make any changes or boundaries, we are actually saying it *is* okay and that we will tolerate it, regardless of how often we voice that we won't.

Our actions reveal our truths. It's okay to give a partner time to change *if* they genuinely want to and are taking the necessary steps to address the concern.

It's also okay if they don't want to change. They can live their life as they please, placing the onus on us to take the necessary steps to work on ourselves, distance ourselves temporarily or potentially leave the relationship.

If we make empty threats without follow through, it is simply manipulation. It may not feel like it. It may feel like honesty and the only way to communicate how serious we are, but no one takes repeated complaints seriously without consequences.

Idle threats subtly communicate to our partner that they don't have to work on themselves, no matter how much we complain, threaten, cry, leave and return. Idle threats lower our happiness ceiling because we are not being true to ourselves and our word.

If we give someone an ultimatum, we must mean it and act on it. If we can't, then we shouldn't issue the ultimatum. The bottom line is we can state our needs in a clear, direct way *one time.* A partner who wants and can show up for us will hear, understand and respond to the message *the first time.*

If we find ourselves repeating our needs over and over, and our partner is not making a genuine effort to address them or respond, the problem isn't with them, it's with us. We want them to change so we don't have to change (or work on ourselves or leave), but they've already told us through inaction that they are not interested in changing. By staying, we are denying their true selves, our true selves and lowering our happiness ceiling. We are not entitled to assume or assert that other people should change to make it easier for us to avoid changing ourselves.

"I am not what you see.
I am what time and effort and interaction slowly unveil."

—Richelle E. Goodrich

CHAPTER FOURTEEN

Get Inspired with Family

Whether we are looking for ways to improve our experience with a new baby, an active toddler, attitude laden teenager, young adult discovering his or her own way, or our parents, we all want the same thing—to be truly seen and accepted by our family members. We don't want to be seen for the choices we made ten years ago, but for who we are today.

Sometimes we don't feel safe enough to share our true selves with our children or parents, making it impossible to truly feel seen by them. We may create a protective barrier if we're judging ourselves or feel judged.

If we developed this protective barrier in our youth, as adults, we can talk with others if we feel we can't share our true selves and see if the response encourages new opportunities for loving connection. We may now be in a more accepting environment where we can work toward breaking down that barrier.

Take a moment to reflect on the members of your family—your kids, spouse, parents, siblings. Who in your family is comfortable sharing their true self with you? Is there anyone you wish you knew better? While you can't control what they show you, you can use inspiration as a way to get to know someone's depth quite easily.

Ask a person, "how was your day?" and you'll likely get the same superficial response. Ask them what they are passionate about, what some of their favorite memories, hobbies or experiences are, and you'll see them light up in an instant. You might not be able to get a word in!

Look for that inspired shift—the moment the same ol' conversation truly gets meaningful, magical and creates an opportunity for true self-expression. It's magical because you can instantly tell when you've tapped into what inspires someone. It's so real, genuine, and a magical pathway to truly connecting.

KIDS

Before kids learn to hide who they are, they are just gushing to show us. We have a powerful choice in how we show love and acceptance as they first discover what they like and don't like, how they communicate and how they discover boundaries. It's a challenge to put our own judgments, personality, and dreams for our children aside to let them lean in to who they truly are. Of course, there must be boundaries and each family may have different values, but to build confident and kind kids, we must celebrate their uniqueness.

How can you celebrate a child's uniqueness? Give them choices so you both can learn what they like, thus allowing them to teach themselves and you who they are. You may think you know the answer, but practice teaching them strategic thinking skills by asking "which one do you want—this one or this one," and practice supporting their decisions without inflicting any doubt or judgment.

TEENAGERS

Can't get your teenager to open up? Stop asking how their day was and starting asking questions that could tap into discovering what inspires them. Who are their role models? What's their favorite song this week? What makes them feel like a rock star? Which friends do they admire? What celebrity would they be right now and why? If they had an extra two hours each day, what would they do? If they could learn a new skill, what would it be?

Kids and teenagers are always changing and growing. Just because you ask a question once, doesn't mean the answer may not be different the next week. And be assured, kids know (as do adults) when we're looking for disingenuous or obligatory shortcuts to get to know them. They also know when you are completely present, sincere, caring, and curious to know who they really are.

More challenging is creating time and opportunity for your teen to express themself without you expressing judgment (directly or indirectly). It's too easy to get sucked into conversations about one of their friend's older boyfriends (that you don't approve of), their desire to wear outfits that you don't like, or their assumed lack of "understanding" about the real world (versus digital interaction).

But none of that is meaningful conversation. Find out *why* the friend likes her new boyfriend, *why* your teen selected that outfit, *why* they enjoy digital conversation and the latest apps. You'll learn more from what they share and how they share it than when you're just going back and forth on the details about judging *what* you like or don't like.

There is no better way to build a connection with your teenager than through being present, genuinely interested in who they truly are, and refraining from judgment as they go through self-discovery.

FAMILY

Whether spending 18 years under the same roof or experiencing all sorts of other arrangements, some folks didn't have a real opportunity to meet their parents' true selves. Some parents never meet their own true selves, making it that much more challenging for us to get to "see" them in the way we want to be "seen" by our parents.

As adult children of our parents, we humanly crave acceptance and love. Whether we received this in abundance or scarcity, or anywhere in between, if we want to connect deeply with our parents or family members, we need to deeply know and understand them.

Maybe they never let their guard down in front of you or didn't show much emotion. Maybe they were so emotional that you couldn't find a core foundation through the series of reactions and chaos. Maybe you want a better relationship with your family members and never understood why that didn't feel possible. Regardless of your circumstances or reasons, if you want to get to know your family better, your best bet is to connect though inspiration.

While each family is different and there are endless arrangements as to what "family" means, if we want to better know someone important in our lives, we all become more open and personal when we get to share what inspires us. You can use the questions in the next chapter to help open new doors for vulnerability and connection.

We may not be able to influence how present our parents or family members can be with us or how freely they will offer their true selves, but we can extend our desire, if authentic, to learn about who they are by connecting with what inspires them. Sometimes, all you have to do is ask the right questions to light up and free one's soul.

*"Curiosity is, in great and generous minds,
the first passion and the last."*

—Samuel Johnson

CHAPTER FIFTEEN

Questions to Discover What Inspires Someone (or Yourself)

Just as we know when we strike a metaphorical nerve with someone, we also know when we tap into what inspires them. Boring talk and simple answers transform into fireworks of enthusiastic stories. Faces noticeably light up. Excitement and energy flow freely between the words.

I remember a meeting I arranged to get to know a potential customer. Over coffee, we were having the usual conversation about business. At some point, one of us mentioned something about a juice cleanse. Suddenly, the energy accelerated. We leaned forward, entering a whole new dimension while we shared the highs and lows of juice cleansing. The remainder of our conversation was focused on shared inspiration, effortlessly letting inspiration carry the conversation forward. In the process, I gained a new customer. And I'm pretty sure it wasn't only the result of our obligatory business talk.

Whether it's a potential new client, a date, or family member, discovering what inspires someone is fun, interesting, and can spark inspiration in us, too. There is a clear, noticeable moment when you can see someone shift from surface conversation into their true selves, enlivening with inspiration.

Here are some questions that can help us tap into getting to know a person's true self. Note that if a response is related to other people rather than the speaker, follow up by asking about something they do or could do alone. For instance, a mother might respond that watching her son play baseball inspires her, which shows her love for being a parent and her admiration for her son. That's a great start. But we can go deeper into the personal part of what inspires her by finding out what she does or could do on her own without it being related to family time. It's easy to lose ourselves in what inspires our children, but it's important we continue to tap into our own inspired secret world that's just for us.

1) If you had two extra hours a day to spend doing something by yourself, what would you do?

2) If you had two extra hours a day to spend doing something with others, what would you do?

3) Where do you want to travel?

4) What are your top three favorite days or experience in life so far?

5) What do you do that makes you smile the most?

6) What's on your bucket list?

7) If you could do anything for three days without physical or financial constraints, how would you spend those three days?

8) What's your favorite view?

9) What's your favorite smell?

10) What do you love doing that you enjoy sharing with or teaching others?

11) Who inspires you and why?
12) If you could wake up tomorrow and live a day in someone else's life, who would it be and why?
13) What do you do that brings you energy?
14) What do you do that makes you feel good about yourself?
15) If you could download five new skills, hobbies, talents, languages, professions, learning them with the click of a button, what would they be?
16) Over what challenges have you triumphed?
17) If you had to spend five minutes looking at an inanimate object, what would it be?
18) In what scenario, real or imaginary, could you imagine yourself feeling completely free?
19) What song have you listened to most in your life and why?
20) Whom or what activity got you through a challenging time?
21) What inspires you to feel positive?

STEP 5:

Break through the 10 Ceilings of Happiness

1. Being Disconnected From Our True Self
2. Trusting Others More Than Ourselves
3. Caring about Others' Happiness More Than Our Own
4. Fear
5. Negative Self-Talk
6. Telling Stories That Limit Ourselves or Others
7. Being Judgmental
8. Avoiding the Truth
9. Feeling Emotionally Exhausted
10. Excuses

*"Even if I knew that tomorrow the world would go to pieces,
I would still plant my apple tree."*

—Martin Luther

CHAPTER SIXTEEN

Symptoms of an Uninspired Life

Often times, we are unhappy when we are out of alignment with ourselves. We may be denying truths because we are afraid or resistant to act in congruence with them or because we have taken a disempowered stance in creating our own life. While all that may require some time to unravel and improve, here's the great news about happiness versus inspiration:

We don't have to be happy to be inspired.

We can label ourselves as generally unhappy and still enjoy bouts of inspiration. We can take breaks from unhappiness without having to do much work!

While I'm a huge proponent of personal work, growth and embracing change, that's not what this book is about. This is about fast-tracking to the inspired life, resulting in true happiness through default.

What does it mean that we can be generally unhappy and still experience inspiration? In short, it means if we're not feeling our best, we don't have to fret about the big picture. We can collect inspired moments as we go along. We don't have to change our lives overnight or put pressure on ourselves to be happy right now or tomorrow. We can just let inspiration easily give us moments of relief until they are bountiful.

If we can't think of what to do to be inspired, then it's time to put some dedicated energy and focus on this task. Perhaps we have neglected ourselves too much, for too long and are disconnected from ourselves. We deserve to remove self-imposed limitations on our lives.

What are symptoms of an uninspired life? The answer is simple. We're not feeling inspired. We're not doing things that inspire us. It's a simple problem with a simple solution! And it sure beats all the hemming and hawing over why we are unhappy. Imagine the depths we must explore in an attempt to change not being happy. But we can become inspired immediately!

If you are not participating in experiences that inspire you, it may be that you are making choices disconnected from your true self. While I am a fan of reflecting on why this is, if you're short on time, go for the low hanging fruit. Start with the easy stuff on your inspiration list, the items that come to you quickly that you have easy access to, and make a plan to do them! Daily or weekly—don't stretch them out too far if you need an inspiration boost. Double, triple or quadruple your number of inspiring experiences.

Most importantly, allow yourself to be completely present and appreciative of your inspiring moments. Soak in and enjoy every molecular detail of the moment. Let inspiration flow through you, and perhaps it will release some of what's blocking you from your true self. The more energy you bring to yourself through being inspired, the more negative energy you can release. The more effort you apply towards making decisions that are best for you, the more you will connect, discover and empower your true self.

"Feel the fear and do it anyway."[1]

—Susan Jeffers

CHAPTER SEVENTEEN

Break through the 10 Ceilings of Happiness

Inspiration can fast track you to true happiness, but it can only take you to the top of your lowest ceiling of happiness. Now that we've started applying the power of inspiration, we must examine ways to expand our capacity to experience true happiness. Let's explore how we can break through these ceilings and live the abundantly happy and inspired life we deserve.

1. BEING DISCONNECTED FROM OUR TRUE SELVES

We've spent a lot of time talking about how important it is to be connected to our true selves and how we can use inspiration to speed up the process, so let's spend a moment understanding how we get disconnected in the first place.

We don't come out of the womb thinking negatively about ourselves or others. We aren't born talking ourselves out of our true needs and wants. We take in the world, exploring, using our senses, and seeking to find the moments that mean something to us.

As we grow up, we become like Velcro, and stuff starts sticking to us. Often times, it might be other people's stuff—their judgments, opinions, behavior, dictations about "rights and wrongs" and "this is how you should think, feel and act," regardless if it's in alignment with our true selves.

It creates layers upon layers, burying our true selves. It can create a labyrinth of faulty analysis and decision making as we try to connect the outside world to our inside selves.

Generally, the longer it takes for us to make a decision, the greater the disconnect between our current experience of life and our true selves. The more layers we take on from others or our environment, the longer it takes us to navigate the labyrinth to get to what our true selves want, think and feel.

How long is your labyrinth? How much opportunity does *the voice* have to talk you into or out of something? We can start to change by becoming aware of when we are not in the driver's seat of our own life.

If we find ourselves back in Velcro mode, we can remind ourselves that we don't need Velcro anymore to figure out who we are, what we think or how we feel.

It's okay if we don't know how we feel in the moment. It doesn't mean we need to rush or force a decision. It doesn't mean someone else should solve it for us. We can take the time we need to discover what's true for us, and getting into an inspired moment can get us out of our heads and into our hearts.

It's also possible we weren't trained to explore and immerse in what inspired us. We can reflect on how encouraged we were as children to participate and practice what inspired us. Were we given support, time and resources to lean into inspiration? If we weren't, regardless of the reason, we may not have confidence to pursue what inspires us. We may not have confidence to get back into something we love if we're now not as good at it as others. We might be intimidated to go back to learn what we need to dive back into what inspires us.

It's never too late to do what we love and live the inspired life. Don't let confidence, embarrassment or fear hold you back. You might be surprised by how supportive people are to those who boldly, and at any expense, pursue their dreams.

2. TRUSTING OTHERS MORE THAN OURSELVES

Without trust, we feel unsafe. Life and people become unpredictable. We anticipate, we fear and we get paralyzed until we determine something definitive. We need to be able to figure out others before we can relax again.

Trust is an illusion. What we communicate to someone when we say, "I trust you" is really that "I trust you to put my best interest first. I expect you to protect me, take care of me and not to hurt me without exception. I expect you not to change your mind after telling me about who you are, what you think, how you feel, and what you intend to do."

What we are really saying when we have to lean on trust in such a black and white way is that, "I don't trust myself to be okay if you don't put my interests first, if you hurt me, don't protect me, or don't take care of me. I want you to sacrifice honoring yourself if it's compromised by me needing you to honor my wants and needs. I don't trust that I'll be okay if you change who you are, what you think, how you feel, or what you intend to do. I expect you not to change in a way that doesn't suit my needs, wants or comfort."

It's impossible to trust people under this definition because it is their job to honor themselves by putting their interests, needs and wants first the majority of the time—just as it's your job to honor yourself the majority of time. This doesn't mean recklessly following every desire without consequences. This doesn't mean not considering or caring about others' feelings. This simply means that sometimes to honor ourselves, we may hurt another's feelings, create circumstances that are uncomfortable for others or create new situations in which someone else doesn't want to adapt. All of that is still not reason enough to not honor ourselves. They will be okay, and so will we.

Taking actions to honor ourselves doesn't provide a crazy loophole to carelessly treat others with disregard. Cheating, lying, and stealing may serve a person's needs, wants or desires, but it is not done through honoring oneself, nor does this provide an excuse to avoid accountability for one's actions. If we become so disconnected from ourselves that we forget, or never learned, how to assert our healthy needs in a timely manner, we may resort to these negative behaviors at our worst.

Marriages don't end simply because a lack of trust exists. Marriages more specifically end because foundational agreements were broken, disrespectful behavior occurred, healthy and honest communication is lacking, or not "being seen or accepted" has ensued for too long. These experiences result in symptoms that can no longer be ignored.

When we feel others have broken our trust, it feels personal. *The Four Agreements* by Don Miguel Ruiz[2] offers useful insight on not taking things personally. "Nothing others do is because of you. What others say and do is a projection of their own reality, their own dream." I encourage you to read his book to be refreshed by his life-changing perspectives.

The only trust we need is that of our own judgment and choices about what is best for us. We can trust that we know what we need, want and feel. We can trust that we will be okay if someone doesn't put our interests first, hurts us, doesn't protect us, or doesn't take care of us. We can trust that if any of these experiences occur when we are adults, we will be able to make a circumstance-based decision on what we need to do about it. We can trust that we will be "okay" no matter what choices we make to honor ourselves and no matter what choices or behaviors others make in our lives. If we do that, we can pursue inspiration and experience life the way we've dreamed.

CHRONIC INDECISIVENESS

One symptom that we trust others more than ourselves is chronic indecisiveness. "Chronic" is an important distinction since some decisions indeed warrant time, strategy and reflection.

The reasons we can't make decisions easily are often fear-based. They include fear of being judged, fear of being "wrong' (judging ourselves, since "right" and "wrong" are nothing more than judgments), fear of other's reactions and feelings (being met with disapproval, rejection or disappointment), and fear of not being "okay" after our decision. None of these revolve around trusting what we truly want, need or desire.

Indecisiveness creates a problem when it results in us living life in slow motion, when we are not pursuing our dreams and when we are operating from a place of fear instead of confidence. We aren't leading our own life if we struggle with knowing and acting on what we want. We may not be authentic with our opinions or we may make choices because we think they are what someone else would want us to do, think or feel.

If we aren't connected to our true selves and "don't know who we are," we look at decisions as a demand that we show who we are when we don't want to and aren't ready. We feel panicked, which makes decisions that much more muddled and difficult. We escalate each decision to feel like a gamble with our identity and self worth because every forced decision becomes an opportunity to be judged, and we're not convinced that we want to show any indications of our identity, whether authentic or fake.

We are afraid we won't be truly "seen" or that we'll be misunderstood, even though we may not know who we are or how to show it. We are afraid someone won't like us or won't approve of us. Worse, when we are not brave enough to show and act as our authentic selves, we may try to portray a fabricated presentation of ourselves to try to earn acceptance.

141

If our fake portrayal of what we think is a "better" version of ourselves is rejected, we can only imagine how much more devastating and hurtful it would be if our true selves, with our authentic opinions and choices, were met with rejection. If we don't think our true self is good enough, what do we have left if the fake version isn't good enough either?

We shut down and allow even less of our true selves to show, which is the opposite of what we truly need and deserve. We begin to bury our true selves, making it harder for others to find or reject us, but also making it harder for us to find ourselves.

Indecisiveness itself doesn't always impede happiness, except if we experience stagnation and lackluster settling for what other people prefer instead of what we'd most enjoy. If indecisiveness is creating a ceiling of happiness for you, it equally provides a solution.

We can use decisions as a way to start discovering our true wants and needs and building strength to let our true selves show.

Start with small opportunities to share what you like and don't like. Start making small decisions in front of other people. Pay attention to times you don't take a definitive opinion on a preference, especially when asked. "Easy going" and flexible can be great attributes, but not if they come at the price of not knowing your true self and taking the easy way out to let others decide for you.

When a friend asks where you want to eat, don't deflect and let the other person choose. Pick your favorite spot or try a completely new one. Every time you make a decision that honors your true self, you are becoming more connected with your true self. You are becoming stronger every time you persevere through the fear of being judged or disapproved. Be comfortable saying no and stating your opinion when you expect someone else to disagree. Practice living life by your choices, even if someone else attempts to reject them. If you have someone in your life that will not like, love or support you for who you are, then they will always be a ceiling on your happiness, and a low one at that.

Celebrate your choices. You don't have to be afraid that your decisions might be "wrong" because there is no one that can determine that for you. No matter how many pros and cons precede, an outcome can never be precisely predicted, and you can handle whatever follows. You will be "okay," and if you start making small and big decisions from your true self, you'll be on a new path to true happiness. You are here on this earth to share *your* unique perspective, enjoy what *you* like and express *your* true self.

LABELING OUR JOURNEY

We face one set of internal challenges when we label other people, but what about when we label our own journey? Using words like "right" and "wrong" are as unhelpful as the *shoulds*.

The only "right path" for you is the one that stems deeply from the core of your true self. The only "wrong" path for you is one that is not in alignment or acting in honor of your true self.

The more you dissolve layers blocking your true self, the faster you can access what really inspires you. The compounding positive effects make it easier to build self-esteem when you're honoring your true self. Your true self is never so lost that you can't find yourself again, and you don't need to label your journey for yourself or anyone else.

3. CARING ABOUT OTHERS' HAPPINESS MORE THAN OUR OWN

When we care more about what others want than we care about what we want, we are destined to have a low ceiling of happiness. This situation may stem from deep-rooted learned behavior that is difficult to simply will away.

Often times, if we are in this space, we think that caring

more about our own feelings, wants, needs or desires is "selfish."

Let's define selfish: "concerned excessively or exclusively with oneself: seeking or concentrating on one's own advantage, pleasure, or well-being without regard for others."[3]

Now let's look at defining selfless: "having no concern for self."[4] Well, that's not so great, either!

Extremes are generally not as healthy as balance. So let's not be *excessively* or *exclusively* concerned with ourselves, but let's also have concern for ourselves.

We can be moderately and generally concerned with ourselves and still exercise regard for others. We can have at least as much concern for our own welfare as we do for the welfare of others. We can consider the point of view of others without letting them make our decisions. We can make final decisions for ourselves from a place of honoring ourselves and still have consideration for others, therefore not being selfish or selfless.

WHEN BEING SELFLESS IS ACTUALLY ALL ABOUT OURSELVES

Being selfless can ironically be completely about ourselves when we come from a place of low self-esteem. We think giving a great amount of service, attention or affection is what someone wants, but they just want to be "seen." We think we are doing a favor by making our world about them, when instead we are just using them to feel better about ourselves, often subconsciously.

Other's can sense when we aren't honoring ourselves, just like we sense when someone isn't honoring themselves. While being doted upon and having our every wish served might feel amazing for a little while, when we sense someone's attachment to us is less about us and who we truly are and more about serving their needs to be validated, needed or wanted, we feel it.

We might entertain this behavior for a while, but we begin to resent that this person, who adores and would go to the moon and back for us, doesn't "see" us. What feels like the world revolving around us, ironically, is not about us at all. It's about them. We could be anyone filling their void or serving their purpose. We feel used, we get resentful, and we may not know why. But we know when we aren't being seen, and it can't be faked for long.

Meanwhile, they are giving everything they have for us, thinking they are the best partner *ever,* but we feel the encumbrance of their low self-esteem.

Low self-esteem is tough on everyone. It's not generous. It's a heavy weight, often shared with those around us. It's loaded with expectations. It's loaded with control.

If we do something that appears to be loving toward another but is really about getting something we want or need, it doesn't make them feel good or us feel fulfilled for long, if at all.

Instead, if we come from a place of loving and honoring ourselves first, our generosity of spirit and acts of kindness mean something real. There's no catch or ulterior motive to get a response. When we're connected to our true selves and another person inspires us enough to make the effort to express gratitude, only then is our loving behavior as real and genuine as it gets. They feel it and can accept it freely.

A SKEWED DEFINITION OF SELFISHNESS

If you struggle with thoughts like, "my decisions will negatively affect others. Living like that is selfish," I recommend looking into codependence. Living your life for others is not living your life. When the flight attendant instructs you to put your oxygen mask on before your child's, it means you have to be at *your* best before you can truly help others.

Honoring yourself is not selfish—it's vital. Are those you think you are accommodating repaying you by equally putting your best interests first? If not, you're likely doing too much for them and can instead do more for yourself. Self-care isn't selfish—it's fundamental to a fulfilling, happy and healthy life.

NOT BEING EMPOWERED TO
CREATE THE LIFE YOU WANT

Consider the following truth: You will not be able to achieve happiness if you are uncomfortable getting your needs met, are not willing to share your true self, or are not willing to pursue your true passions because you're afraid of judgment or failure.

You can get inspired under these circumstances, but you deserve more than a ceiling on your happiness. These learned behaviors may take time, resources and commitment to change, but you deserve it! You are solely responsible for creating the life you want, and you have access to every tool you need to do so. You deserve to live your most inspired life without this ceiling of happiness blocking the life you want.

4. FEAR AND WORRYING

Fear and worrying are closely related, both placing formidable ceilings on our happiness. It's one thing when our instincts are warning us about a dark alley when we are alone, but most fear is based on future events that may or may not happen. Fear is not being present. Fear is trying to predict or control an outcome that you may not have influence over. You will be okay, and the outcome will be what it is regardless of how much you worry, obsess or plan. In fact, you'll be more level headed and influential if you stay present.

I used to have to know an outcome. I obsessively sifted through every possible outcome I could predict so that I could do my best to "prepare" for the feelings and consequences to come. This was all based on not feeling in my core that I was going to be okay.

How did it serve me to worry about things before they

happened? The act of obsessively thinking through every option so I could "know" my options was more predictable, made me feel like I had some control (which is delusional), and set me up to try to manipulate an outcome.

I thought by proving I was really "doing something" about the potential issue, it would be less likely to happen because of "fairness." Part of me thought, "Will I deserve a good outcome if I don't really worry or obsess about it? If I don't prove that I am really concerned about this potential problem, will it be more likely to slip through the cracks and into my life? Will it happen more easily if I don't put up a fight?"

In hindsight, I can see the ridiculousness of my thoughts and convictions, but at the time it was all I had to hold onto: the hope that someone, or God, or the Universe would see how much I really didn't want this to happen, and that my worry would be enough to convince this force not to proceed.

I never had any control over these situations, but pretending like I did seemed like the only chance I had at protecting myself from being unhappy.

Now I know that I will be okay, and that it's okay to feel sad or angry or hurt. It won't last forever, and I have inspiration by my side to uplift me when these feelings arise.

I used to be a little superstitious. I made wishes on shooting stars and I held my breath through tunnels. I ensured I blew out a candle on my actual birthday because "that's when it had the most power" to make my wish come true.

While, admittedly, I still get some nostalgic joy from these practices, after some major life changes a few years ago, I had an epiphany: What if all my wishes in those moments had come true?

In hindsight, I don't think I would have been as happy as I thought in the moments I made those wishes. I would have married the wrong guy before I learned how destructive my codependency was. I would have missed out on so many amazing experiences I couldn't have predicted.

And that's the point. We really don't know. I'm a huge advocate for working towards our dreams, using confidence and determination to ask for what we want in life. But I also would have given everything I owned to marry Phil Collins when I was eight years old. I definitely spent a lot of wishes on Phil Collins over the years because he inspired me, and apparently as an eight year old, I needed to marry my inspiration to keep it forever.

Even though I still make wishes, I wish differently. Even though I believe we can manifest what we want by extending energy with that intention, I also believe in what spiritual leader and personal inspiration source, Iyanla Vanzant, says: "You will never miss out on what is meant for you, even if it has to come to you in a roundabout way."[5] I have had enough experiences to look back and see how not getting what I wanted ended up so much better than I could have imagined.

The challenges we face, the big ones and little ones, are just continuing us on our path, and we can't see what's around the corner. Different religions and philosophies have their own way of messaging this concept, but the basis is that trying to control outcomes is useless. Nevertheless, we aren't helpless in creating our life story.

Pursue what inspires you, ask for what you want, and when you get a "no," trust that you will be okay. There is something else waiting for you that you would have missed out on if all our wishes came true when you made them.

PRE-EXPERIENCING TO NO AVAIL

Why do we worry? We're scared. We're bored. We need something to do or something to think about. We worry about what we already did. What he or she did. We worry about the future. Either way, we don't trust that we'll be okay. We feel safe thinking we've obsessed about every possibility so that we are prepared. We don't want to experience discomfort, and yet we're ironically inflicting discomfort in order to try to avoid it.

What are we afraid of? Being unhappy. Being uncomfortable or sad or mad or scared or alone. If we anticipate and practice the feelings that we are hoping to avoid, we essentially are already experiencing these feelings as if they are real.

As reported by Calm Clinic, "Adrenaline is one of the most common causes of anxiety symptoms. Your body releases it when your fight or flight system is active, and it causes the increase in heart rate, muscle tension, and more. In some cases, long term stress and anxiety may damage your ability to control adrenaline, leading to further anxiety symptoms."[6]

If we are anticipating and role playing to practice handling a scenario, if we activate our fight or flight response, then we are pre-experiencing the exact stress that we are trying to avoid.

Absurdly, we are choosing to feel unhappy because we're afraid of possibly being unhappy later. How silly we can be!

How do we stop worrying? By not worrying about worrying!

THOUGHT SUPRESSION DOESN'T WORK

Trying to suppress thoughts actually keeps what you're trying to suppress more top of mind.

The psychological principal of ironic thought suppression is that the more we suppress thoughts or try not to think about them, the more they are present. Consider this excerpt about a thought suppression experiment, shared by Ira Hyman Ph.D. from his article, "Don't Think About It:"

"Erskine and Georgiou conducted an experiment in which they looked at the effects of suppressing thoughts of chocolate. First, participants engaged in a task of recording their thoughts. One-third were asked to think about chocolate, one-third to suppress thoughts of chocolate, and one-third to simply record their thoughts with no suggestions about content. Later all participants were asked to rate some chocolate on several qualities related to taste. The issue was not their ratings, but rather how much chocolate they ate. People who had tried to suppress thoughts about chocolate ate more chocolate! Suppression not only led to a rebound in chocolate thoughts, but also to a rebound in eating chocolate."[7]

Here are some examples of how the ironic thought process works, excerpted from the article, "5 Ways Your Brain Is Tricking You into Being Miserable" by Kathy Benjamin and Dieter Melsens:

"Psychologists call these ironic thought processes. They are the reason why you only want the stuff that you can't have, why trying to suppress laughter only makes you laugh more, why you fail at stuff when somebody is watching, and so on. Telling yourself not to be afraid of failure puts failure right at the center of your thoughts. It's the difference between overweight people who are always counting calories and rail-thin people who have to be reminded to eat at meal time because otherwise they just 'forget to eat.' The overweight dieters are constantly failing because staying under the calorie count requires them to do the one thing they should be avoiding: thinking about food."[8]

So if we aren't supposed to think, or worry, about not having chocolate, happiness or positive self-talk, what are we supposed to think about? We might try to distract ourselves from the present by providing ourselves some kind of temporary escape. But it's far more healing and recharging to find distraction in the present—in an inspired moment.

We don't have to try to suppress our judgments about being unhappy. We don't have to bother with happiness at all. We can fill our time and thoughts with inspired moments and let the rest take a break for a while.

If we do this enough, we won't have time to worry. We'll be too busy being inspired in the present to remember how much we're supposed to think about the past or future. This is the new norm we want for our brain, and if we practice this mindset enough, inspiration instead of worry can become our default.

Today, right now, choose to change your mindset about worrying. Choose inspiration as your coping skill. Seek information if you need to, but don't worry; worrying is just unnecessary, unhelpful and self-imposed stress.

Trying to prepare for an outcome by pre-experiencing it will not change if it will happen, when it will happen, or how it will happen. Trust that if whatever you're worrying about comes to fruition, you will have access to the necessary strength and courage—qualities that you already possess, but that may not be realized until they are needed.

We are capable of astounding resiliency if we free ourselves to let it flow and release our unfriendly "crutch" of worrying.

5. NEGATIVE SELF-TALK

The worst role *the voice* plays is negative self-talk. Internal dialogue feeding us with negative self-talk is something we have to change to live a happier life.

Can you imagine if we were capable of judging ourselves when we were babies? "I'm so fat, look at this pudge. It's gross. I should put a shirt on; People can't even tell if I'm a boy or a girl, how embarrassing; I am not good at anything except eating. Why would anyone want me around? I'm useless; my smile is so gummy. I don't think I'll smile until my teeth come in. I'll just keep my mouth closed to hide how messed up my gums and teeth are."

A baby being self-conscious about smiling? That is a heartbreaking notion. We were free of self-judgment when we were babies, and yet at some point, we developed a sensitivity that taught us to react with self-consciousness and negative self-talk.

You didn't make up those negative thoughts all by yourself. Where do those words come from? When did the negativity develop? Whose voice was echoing in your head until you made it your own?

The negative self-talk voice is extremely destructive and likely won't go away on its own without some real effort. That voice will talk you out of being inspired, doing things that inspire you, or knowing what inspires you. That voice may be the lowest ceiling for your happiness, and you deserve an infinite sky above you.

If you wouldn't say those things to someone else you love, why are you saying them to yourself? If you were in a room with yourself as a kid, would you say those words looking into the eyes of an innocent child bursting to share who they are with you, deserving of kindness, love and acceptance? Frame a childhood photo or carry one around if you want to remind yourself of how kind you would be to that fragile soul. You are still bursting with desire to share your true self and are worthy of kindness, love and acceptance, and this practice may help you re-connect with the pure human-ness we all share that needs nurturing.

You have to stand up to that internal bully and possibly to those who were externally part of creating that voice. You have to advocate for yourself and prove to yourself that you deserve better.

Beginning to have awareness around how often you have negative self-talk will help you start to separate it from your usual self. Replacing it with positive self-talk and positive affirmations is one step in practicing different behavior until it becomes more of a default. You'll be building confidence by letting inspiration be positive self-expression. Counseling can also provide extra guidance and support to break through this low ceiling of happiness.

These choices and tools can all help you speak more lovingly to yourself as you would want someone to speak to those you love in your life, including yourself.

6. TELLING STORIES THAT
LIMIT OURSELVES OR OTHERS

Humans have always been storytellers. From early ancient writings in caves to today's social media frenzy, we use stories to share who we are and who we want to be. But what about the stories that depict who we *were*, but that really don't apply anymore? What about the ceilings we put on other people, needing to define others in a black or white way for us to have more control and understanding of who they are?

STORIES FROM OUR PAST

We too easily put boundaries on defining who we are. While hardships some of us faced as children helped to shape us, likely in both positive and negative ways, they do not have to limit who we are today.

We tell our stories to get people to understand us and what we've been through. But often, when we tell these stories over and over again to ourselves and others, we begin to label and identify ourselves as victims. We may have been victims then, but we choose to remain victims if we allow everything in our life to reinforce these stories.

We stay stuck in these stories and allow life to further prove that our stories remain true. For example, if we learn early in life that we can't trust people, we might subconsciously continue to fill our life with untrustworthy people. We can then say, "See, I was right!"

If we've only dated jerks or manipulative women, we tell the story that all men or women are like that, and we attract more of the same because it's what we know. While we may be sad or mad about the partners we choose, it is always our choice. We settle for what's familiar and comfortable. Sadly, what feels familiar, comfortable and safe can also feel sad, lonely or unhappy.

We might want to change these feelings by attracting a different partner, but we have to change first and work through why these feelings became familiar and comfortable in the first place.

Without foundational work to shift our personal norms, we may miss out on relationships with people who would prove our story wrong. We know we want a kind, honest and supportive partner, but we may not know how to interact or respond emotionally to foreign behavior, so we revert back to our tainted view of our past so we can stay in our comfort zone and continue to tell our story. Because, without our story, we don't know who we are.

Let's pretend we have a recurring dream in which we're plunked down on the side of a desert highway. We know we have to get to the next town, so we start walking. It's hard, we're not getting our needs met, and if we could just get to the next town quickly, we could rest our tired feet, get some water and enjoy a meal.

As we're walking along, we come across a functioning abandoned car with the key in the ignition (this is clearly a dream). We get inside and discover it's a manual stick shift, which we never learned how to drive.

Instead of struggling to figure it out, we go back to our same long and treacherous walk, and don't think much about how helpful it would have been if we only knew how to drive a stick shift. This long walk is what we know, and as tired as we are, it's comfortable. It's our story.

We have this dream over and over, and it's always the same. We never learn how to drive a stick shift because once we get to our destination, we're happy! We get our rest, food and water. And we get to share how difficult and exhausting that journey was. Our dream, which represents any experience in our lives that we feel seems to be repeating in ways we don't want, will repeat until we do something to change it. Lessons repeat until we change and grow from them. Since we are the common thread in the relationships and circumstances in our lives, recurring themes in our lives won't change unless we personally change something first.

We know our past really well, and we've been practicing our stories for years, but we're not leaving room for the present to be different from our past. We think we want something different, but we don't know how to get it.

The metaphorical dream example, that you kindly entertained, represents how we repeat patterns until we take the time to learn something different so we can do something differently, and therefore experience different results. If our relationships seem to unfold and end with a similar pattern or we're facing repetitive experiences that we don't want, we have to stop before we get caught up in another round; we need to learn how to drive that stick shift. If deep down we want to change our story, we have to take the time and do the work to change our role in the story.

Why don't we want to change our stories? Because healing can be hard, forgiveness can be harder, and accepting truths around these experiences can be the most heartbreaking part of all. But we shouldn't be victims of the same story forever. We owe it to our adult selves to move on and re-write our story. If we start living the story we *want* to be true, we'll attract what or who we need to make it true. If we change what we believe, we will change our reality.

Don't let your past determine your future. Your past can be a stepping-stone instead of defining your entire path. Let go of past beliefs that might once have been true that don't have to be true anymore. Believe you can define your life and yourself as so much more than any ceiling you were born under.

STORIES ABOUT OTHER PEOPLE

It's too easy to use another's perceived faults or weaknesses to make ourselves feel better. I never realized how much I did this (how awful, right? No "nice" person would do this!) until I tapped into the storytelling I did about others.

For me, it seemed innocent enough. I was simply telling true accounts of behavior or situations I witnessed, whether to myself or out loud. But in actuality, I was telling stories about people that affirmed the box I put them in, the label I gave them and the ceiling I put them under. If it didn't reinforce the label, I didn't add it to the story to create dimension. If it didn't fit my story about them, I threw it out like it never happened and didn't exist.

The problem with needing to make sense of someone in such a definitive way is that it is delusional. It simply isn't true for any of us. We feel safer when we can label someone and figure them out, but it's hardly foolproof. "Good people" are capable of bad behavior. "Bad people" are capable of good behavior.

We can assess a partner or parent or stranger as a "good person," therefore ignoring or justifying any "bad" behavior. We don't hold them accountable or even acknowledge it. We might tell stories that someone is ignorant or incompetent, not giving credit for instances where this does not prove true. We throw out their behavior as a fluke or ignore it because it doesn't fit our label or story about them. The problem is that we still process the truth on a soul level, and then subconsciously we don't know what to do other than to bury it.

To clean this up, we have to be comfortable accepting the complexity of humans, especially those who have influence in our lives. We might be creating a more surface relationship to protect our story rather than the truth. Being able to see one another for our brightest and darkest facets is how we are truly seen and can make deep connections. It's also how we make decisions to detach from unhealthy relationships that are putting a ceiling on our own potential for health and happiness.

We miss out on true connections when we choose to only see and reinforce the "good" or "bad" aspects to keep our story straight. It's important to be forever curious about discovering the endless facets of who other people are, as we are generally forever discovering the endless facets of who we are as individuals. We are all changing, some moving farther away from our true selves and some moving closer. The stories we tell likely only capture a few of our many facets in a moment in time.

Most of my experience telling stories wasn't based on labeling people "good" or "bad" specifically. My proclivity was to not honor another's ability to have duality in general. One failed attempt doesn't mean someone can't succeed on another attempt. One emotional reaction doesn't mean every decision is void of strategy. Even if half the information we process "about" someone tells us something, it doesn't mean they can't surprise us at any time with positive or negative behavior we can't predict.

Telling stories that are based on a convenient attachment to selected moments instead of the spectrum of witnessed truths is only telling a story about who we are. We can allow others to be capable of "good" and "bad" behavior, to make "smart" decisions and decisions that don't produce the desired outcome, and to have moments of weakness and moments of strength. We can release our need to attach labels and judgments to people in order for us to feel safer or better able to predict the behavior of others.

ACCEPTING COMPLEXITY DOESN'T MEAN ACCEPTING ALL BEHAVIOR IN OUR LIVES

The stories we tell, in this context, may be exaggerated and biased either positively or negatively, but they are equally dangerous because they are both rooted in a denial of truth. Even though accepting the complex nature of humans is an important component of stopping our story telling, it doesn't result in having to accept all behavior in our lives.

Not telling stories doesn't mean we can't distance ourselves from people whose behavior generally hasn't been kind to us. If their behavior becomes kind in the future, we can decide to reconnect in a way that feels best for us as we see circumstances change.

We don't have to allow someone in our lives if they aren't coming from a loving and symbiotic intention for a relationship. We know kind and loving actions when we feel them, and we know when someone is interacting with us because they truly care about us or when they are using us.

We can evaluate our involvement in a relationship with someone who is intentionally dishonest, not honoring relationship agreements, or not proving they carry integrity with their word.

We can trust our judgment as circumstances and people change (or don't) to live in the flow of life without labels, stories or limitations. It's okay to let others earn our love, time and respect. We are all capable of offering a kind, loving, honest, respectful and symbiotic relationship, and no one is entitled to treat us poorly and then expect unconditional love and respect in return.

7. BEING JUDGMENTAL

Being judgmental can be closely related to the stories we tell about others.

Someone once told me I was really judgmental. I felt like I should be offended, and I was definitely confused. Isn't it good to be judgmental? Don't we use judgment to make good decisions? Isn't it true that someone chooses to look or act a certain way as a means of expressing who they are and how they want me to see them?

There I was thinking I was being a strategic thinker in taking subtle (or not so subtle) cues from people about what they are trying to tell me about themselves. (Are you sensing me trying to label someone so that "I've figured them out" and can avoid living with the ambiguity of human nature?)

I decided to dive into understanding what being judgmental is and why it is not "good." After much reading and research, I determined for myself that being judgmental requires two components being activated at the same time:

1) Making a determination about who someone "is;" thinking we can predict how they think or how they will act

   2) Thinking that I am better than this person because I have made or would make decisions differently, resulting in a "better" outcome

The second one is the clincher for me. While a part of me still uses the first as way to use my judgment (that lone man lurking in the parking garage, wearing a black trench coat, might be dangerous because of how he looks), the second component is my self-imposed red flag to put myself in check.

I thought I did a *lot* of things better than other people. I didn't get to be a "kid" for long. I developed a proactive and heightened sense of awareness, strong intuition, and quick strategic mind before many kids would have to build or use these life skills. I had to pay attention to people and situations in a way those enjoying an easier childhood did not. For me, it was necessary to my interpretation of survival.

As an adult, in the workplace, these qualities could be an asset; but personally, they posed a problem. After developing rapid analytical and decision-making skills ahead of some of my peers, and continuing to fine tune that part of my brain as I got older, what if I really did think I did, or would, make better decisions that would result in a better outcomes? What if I felt I could better predict an outcome, or I'd already learned "that" lesson, or I'd paid more proactive attention to the circumstances and could provide an educated guess faster than someone else?

The *"I"* in these questions represents the emphasis of my lesson to learn. I was taking someone else's life and pretending it was mine. All I actually know is perhaps *I* could make a better decision for *me*—for *my life*.

To avoid being judgmental, I focus my experience and intuition on how I would solve my own problems, not how someone else should solve theirs. I acknowledge that what serves me well in my life may not equally serve someone else.

"Better" is one of those judging words, which is generally subjective. I don't know another person's circumstances, fears, background, capacity, goals, or what best serves them in their life. In short, *I might make a better decision for myself*, but who am I to determine if it's also better for someone else?

What I learned is that I was often using my judgments as a way to tolerate the passiveness I perceived in others. I'm not afraid to be decisive, bold, or make changes. When I'm around others who aren't as comfortable being so direct, decisive, curious or proactive, I get annoyed and impatient because I can't relate to prolonging certain results of what I (subjectively) see as truths that will play out sooner or later. I can't relate to not being curious about the most efficient or cost-effective way to do something.

My coping mechanism relies on that second component of judgment, which is all about me and what *I* can handle, not about the person I'm judging. It's okay if I would make a different decision to serve my needs or life, but I can't make that decision for someone else because I'm not running their life.

I'm not proud of this trait, but I am aware of it and I work on it.

We can use judgment to justify or cover up other parts of ourselves. We can use judgment to keep telling a good story about ourselves and a bad story about someone else.

We don't need to make our life experience applicable to anyone else. We can question ourselves when we notice we are being judgmental by asking how it is serving us.

AM I BEING JUDGMENTAL OR HELPFUL?
Being helpful not only serves others, it often serves us as well. A *Friends*[9] episode humorously pointed this out when Phoebe could not complete a true act of selfless kindness because of how good she felt afterward or how she benefitted from each one. So let's put altruism off the table for this exploration. We can do good things for other people and get

something from it, and it doesn't discount the positive impact we made in another's life. Of course, this is only if we are coming from a place of honoring ourselves (and not codependence or giving help where it's not needed or requested).

So how do we know when we are being judgmental instead of helpful? When we start using the word *"should."* We throw it around pretty carelessly. "You should totally buy that," "you should call her," or "you should do it this way." We're subtly making something about the other person when it's really about us trying to make ourselves more pleased, comfortable or in control.

Instead, we can reframe our message to be more honest and less manipulative. "I like how you look in that," "I would feel better if you call her," or "I do it like this and I would prefer you to do it the same way." Alternately, "have you ever worn something like this?" "Have you ever done it this way?"

We don't have to go overboard on monitoring *shoulds* when it's said casually ("we should have chicken for dinner"), but it's worth reflection when we find ourselves giving advice and throwing around the *should.*

We can take inventory of our motivations. If they are more about us than them, we can try a quick re-word to infuse ownership and honesty in what we're saying. "I find it efficient to do it like this if you want to try," instead of, "You should do it like this."

Even though it may seem like semantics, it really does make a difference in the internal space that we are coming from and how the other person receives our message. Our words are powerful. If we don't take the time to not be careless with how we say our *shoulds,* we can miss important opportunities to connect with ourselves through speaking our truths.

But that's the easy part of *should.* The hard part stems from the *shoulds* we put on ourselves. Here comes *the voice*! I shouldn't eat that, I should exercise more, I shouldn't like this, I should call her, I should be able to do this, I should look like this, I should blah blah blah.

Shoulds are a form of self-judgment and sometimes a form of negative self-talk or self-rejection. *Shoulds* say what we want for ourselves or what someone else wants of us, but they are not based on who we are at the present time. This dialogue ends with a dip in self-esteem because we aren't where we "should" be or who we "should" be. Says who?

The *should* may be what we really want for ourselves. Maybe we truly want to wake up early every morning to exercise, but we're having trouble getting into that habit. Before we go to bed, we'll likely tell ourselves that we *should* get up early. And if we don't rise and shine with our alarm the next morning, we might spend the day saying we *shouldn't* have slept in.

There is a big, intentional difference between "I should" and "I will." *Shoulds* already have a built in "I might not," letting us off the hook in exchange for guilt and shame.

Internally using the word *should* can lessen the simplicity of commitment and will power. If we confuse our "I will" accountability with a *should,* it's easier to focus on guilt and shame. And now that we're moping around all day with our guilt and shame, we have a distraction from focusing on the confidence and empowerment we need to commit with an "I will" to execute our goal.

If we aren't in a place to make changes we want, then we don't have to judge ourselves for that. We don't have to punish ourselves. We can take ownership of our true selves.

If you're on a diet, you might say, "I shouldn't eat this donut," but go deeper into owning what you really want. If you really want to lose weight, rephrase to say, "I want to lose weight so I will not eat this donut today, even though I really want it." If you've been working hard and want a break, then own that. "I've been doing well on my diet, but today I want a donut because I enjoy it. I'm going to really enjoy it, because after this I'm back to working on my goal."

If, instead, we're telling ourselves we should get up early to exercise so that other people will see us as being strong-willed or thinner, now we're being double judged! The worst part of using the perceived judgment of others coupled with our own self-judgment is that we'll be half-committed to our goal because it's not even something we truly want or want enough to change.

We'll exert just "enough" effort to make it look like we are addressing it because society or people tell us that we *should*. If we're only half committed, we're doing more harm than good and we're setting ourselves up for negative consequences.

Leading with *shoulds* furthers our story that we have low self-control and we are not good enough to reach our goals, when in fact we only halfway committed because it's something we don't fully want or aren't fully ready to pursue.

If we can't connect with what we truly want and make decisions in honor of that, the *shoulds* will let anything slide. They're laced with a lack of accountability, are a disconnect with our truths, and are rigged with a self-esteem destroyer. Rephrasing to be more direct and truthful about our experiences, wants, needs and desires *does* matter, even if it's only to ourselves. Practice, and let go of judging and shaming yourself.

Maybe our *should* is reflecting something we really don't want, but we think someone else wants for us. Maybe the *should* is keeping us from pursuing what our true selves really want. "I should major in pre-med because that's what's expected of me. That's where I'll make money and make my family proud." But if we really want to major in creative writing, we will half commit to pre-med, likely struggle and wonder why we're not happy or inspired.

Who cares that it may not have a guaranteed job path or make as much money. Pursue what inspires you, and never let a *should* prove that you're disconnected from your true self or putting someone else's wants, needs or desires above your own, especially when it comes to your life!

Lastly, those who are judgmental often think everyone is equally judgmental. It almost becomes a defense mechanism. But what if everyone isn't that judgmental? You don't have to be either. You don't need to judge others to "figure" them or yourself out. Free yourself from being judgmental and break through that ceiling of happiness!

8. AVOIDING THE TRUTH

The purity of happiness we experience will always be relative to how freely we can embrace truth. The truth is the truth, regardless of whether we see it, acknowledge it, or act on it. While one's truth may differ from another, avoiding truth will keep true happiness at bay.

I used to think the saying, "the truth will set you free," meant you'll feel less guilty if you don't lie. Today, I realized that the phrase really means that only when we live in truth, can we live freely as our true selves.

Oftentimes we think acknowledging the truth will make us unhappy, so we avoid it. When we acknowledge some truths, we may be unhappy in the short term, but we can heal and accept this outcome. If we avoid the truth, it will impact the purity of the happiness we experience. When we know we are delaying the consequences of truth, whether buried in our subconscious or ignored by our conscious thoughts, our denial continues to steal our potential for true happiness.

When we accept the temporary and surface happiness we achieve by avoiding uncomfortable truths as "good enough," two things occur: 1) we inherently accept that we are not worthy of being truly happy; and 2) we perpetuate the idea that we are not strong enough to be "okay" facing the truth.

Both are our own doing and keep us in a fear-based life with a low ceiling of happiness. Every moment we choose to bury a truth, our true self knows. We have a constant subconscious reminder that we don't believe in ourselves enough. If we are in a fear-based place, then we are not in the present. And if we aren't experiencing life in the present, we aren't inspired!

So let's reverse this flow of thinking to produce a different outcome. The more we practice being inspired, the more we practice being in the present and connecting with ourselves. Hopefully, we gain some confidence through discovering and honoring our true self, which helps us to know we are "okay" with truth.

Once we are okay with truth and have practiced being present, we won't settle for less because we know we deserve to lift our ceiling of happiness, which culminates in greater confidence, greater enjoyment of life, and greater happiness.

Pure happiness starts in the core of our true selves as a constant, a guidepost, a default, and a strength that shines from the inside out. Because the core of our true selves doesn't change or waver with every challenge life presents, neither does our root happiness.

What we practice, we repeat. If we practice making decisions that don't honor ourselves, we forget the potential we have to do so. If we practice ignoring truths and dishonoring ourselves, we get farther away from living a happy life. It might feel like we are just living life as usual, but we are actually getting more and more disconnected.

If we practice being empowered, strong and authentic, it becomes easier to be empowered, strong and authentic. Starting now, make decisions that honor your truth and yourself, and prepare to experience the really good stuff—pure happiness!

9. FEELING EMOTIONALLY EXHAUSTED

If we are too disconnected from ourselves or in relationships in which we are more attached to an outcome or appearance instead of honoring ourselves and our truths, we may feel exhausted. This is not the same as being physically exhausted from being up with a sick kid all week or mentally exhausted from a challenging deadline at work.

We can feel emotionally exhausted if we are not connected to our true selves and working far too hard to maintain the appearance of who we are without being authentic. When we allow ourselves to remain in an environment, situation or relationship that we don't want to change but that is not in alignment with our true selves, we feel exhausted.

Sometimes, this can feel like drama, which I define as unnecessary and sometimes repetitive emotional distress lacking in a commitment to purpose or resolution. Whether you are stuck in your personal state of drama or provide the ear in someone else's drama, the unnecessary stress endured by all involved is a distraction from a genuine interest in achieving true happiness.

The closer we are in alignment to our true selves, the easier life is. The farther we are from being in alignment with our true selves, the more effort each day is. We are trying to fit a square peg into a round hole. We have to put forth effort to proceed through life trying to show or prove who we are because we are not actually honoring who we are, and that effort results in feeling exhausted.

For example, if your car has a flat tire, you can still drive it, but it takes more effort and time for the car get from point A to point B. It might even cause some damage along the way.

Likewise, when we are disconnected from our true selves, our life journey takes more effort and can damage other parts of ourselves. The ride isn't smooth; it's clunky, and we are slower to realize our dreams. We may not know we have a flat tire if our journey's been clunky, slow and challenging for too long. But when we feel exhausted too often, we know something is out of whack. The problem is that we pretty much know when we have a flat tire, but we don't always know that we're disconnected from ourselves.

When we feel emotionally exhausted, we have an

opportunity to reflect on why life is so much effort. Living life connected to our true selves still has challenges, but we move freely, addressing them as they come.

If we find ourselves being emotionally defensive about who we are or the decisions we make, it may be because we are trying to prove something instead of solidly believing our decisions are in alignment.

The more energy we exert to prove who we are or defend our decisions, the less connected we are to ourselves. The longer the story we use to explain every aspect behind our decisions, the less confident we are in our decision. The louder our voice to proclaim who we are, the smaller we feel. We are no longer proving to others, but proving to ourselves.

We don't have to shout from the rooftops who we are if we know who we are—we just are. People will know from our actions and presence, and if that isn't enough for anyone, we might want to re-evaluate the environment or relationship.

We have *the voice* in our heads narrating our day, but when that voice is spoken to others, it's just showing us how disconnected we really are. Just like we don't need *the voice* to know who we are, how we feel or what we want if we are closely connected to our true selves, when we use our voice to narrate who we are to others, it's indicating an insecure and unstable distance between being connected to ourselves. Instead of doing the work to become closer connected to ourselves and facing the consequences of those decisions, we are exerting more energy to talk around it.

If we're often defensive, it means we aren't feeling seen or understood in the way we want, and there are only three reasons for this: 1) We are too far disconnected from our true selves and that unstable or insecure distance is showing up; 2) We have become more connected to ourselves, but haven't broken old patterns of relating to others as our new self; or 3) We are in a dysfunctional relationship with someone (at work, a friendship, family member or love interest) who isn't interested in truly seeing us, and we're trying to change that and force approval.

Being defensive is emotionally exhausting, and there are solutions to every cause. 1) Get more connected and therefor more self-confident (through inspiration, of course!); 2) practice pausing before reacting and allow ourselves to show who we are instead of insist who we are; or 3) change or distance ourselves from those that are trying to keep us as our old selves, likely so they don't have to change their story or adapt.

Another surefire way to feel exhausted is if we hinge our happiness on other people's happiness. We are placing our happiness, something so precious, on someone else's roller coaster of life! Since we can't control other people, we work hard to influence them. It feels like work to earn that happiness. Feeling exhausted is a sure sign that a situation is not in alignment with your true self.

EXHAUSTING RELATIONSHIPS

Another situation that can result in feeling overwhelmed or emotionally exhausted is staying in a relationship that causes us to be disconnected from ourselves. The delicate balance of compromise, *shoulds*, and keeping someone else's needs, feelings and desires in mind can get tricky.

Compromising and being mindful of our partner's needs, feelings and desires while continuing to honor ourselves is important. But, when we get too flexible, compliant, or fearful of upsetting or losing our partner by speaking or acting on our truths and honoring our needs, we are no longer an equal. Our partner knows when he or she can overpower us to get their needs met, even if it's not with malicious or unloving intent.

If we teach people how to treat us by what we allow, our words don't matter if they are unmatched by our actions. Let your actions honor you, and teach your partner that your needs are as important as theirs.

I was once in a relationship with an alcoholic. At the time,

I didn't know what that meant or how it was affecting me. To me, it was a normal relationship with both challenges and beautiful moments. I was always trying to get his attention because he wasn't often present with me. The more I was attached to us being together, the less connected I became to myself.

I was always second to what he wanted, and I allowed it. I didn't want to lose him, so I lost myself instead. I verbalized how unfair it was. I justified the relationship to friends and family. I defended him to myself and others because he had had such a hard life. But understanding why he acted the way he did didn't mean I had to accept it—though I did for two years.

I used my words to prove who I was to him, to state what I wanted, needed and deserved from a partner. But he knew everything I said didn't matter. I wasn't proving it to him; I was trying to prove it to myself. I said I deserved better, but I allowed everything to continue as usual. I wasn't acting in a manner of self-respect, no matter how I stated, yelled or pleaded. I wanted those words, even in conflict with my actions, to be enough so that I didn't have to face the consequences. I didn't act in honor of myself because I didn't want to lose him.

Why do we lose ourselves to avoid losing another? Because we are disconnected from ourselves. The connection cord is too long, thin and frail; we no longer know who we are without that other person. We don't know what we are worth. Without that person, we don't know what we'll have left or what we'll have to offer. We allowed our love for ourselves to be replaced by the love from another, and if we lose that, we will have nothing.

After a lot of personal work, I found myself and let him go. I became so closely connected to myself that I knew I would never again lose myself for someone else. No one's love for me is ever more important than the love I now give myself.

Actions do speak louder than words. If our actions aren't creating boundaries that protect our ability to both honor ourselves and assert our needs and wants as equally important as our partner's, we will seek other ways to persuade, manipulate or cajole to get what we want. Using indirect ways to communicate our needs allows us to avoid the direct and firm assertion we need to make. Navigating these roundabout attempts to be seen and to honor our true selves is exhausting.

We aren't trying to make our relationship work; we are trying to make being disconnected from ourselves look and feel like being connected to ourselves. We might be trying to prove it to ourselves, our partner or our friends and family. We are working so hard to make it look like we are connected when we aren't because the stakes of honoring ourselves seem too high. We have to start being who we truly are and let the chips fall where they may. We can't experience true connection without starting from our true selves, and a person worthy of our partnership will celebrate all that we have to offer.

10. EXCUSES

Excuses are just *the voice* of fear getting in the way of our dreams. We can talk ourselves out of anything and everything if we let fear have a voice.

When we try something new, we probably won't be good at it. No matter what opinion we have, there will always be someone who disagrees. No matter how we do something, there will always be someone who does it differently. What if we choose to accept that being different makes us interesting, that trying something new is brave, and that we don't need everything to be perfect to have a fulfilling life?

The silver lining of struggling, and one reason to not let excuses stand in our way, is that the most inspiring experiences are usually the anomalies. Inspiration will more likely stem from times of overcoming struggle, which means we have to experience struggle in the first place.

For example, who inspires you more? The singer who moves to Nashville and gets a record deal after her first open mic night? Or the singer that moves to Nashville, works three different odd jobs, plays at thousands of open mic nights, bars, and street corners, gets a record deal, gets dropped half way through, waits outside of a different record label for three days playing on the street until they finally decide to sign a final successful record deal?

The singer could make a million excuses to keep her from her dream because it didn't come easy. She could say she's not good enough, doesn't have enough money, isn't cute enough, should do something with more stability, or should go back home.

We aren't as inspired by the Nashville singer that's handed a contract on her first day compared to the one who challenged herself through a twisty pathway of unknowns to reach her dreams.

We aren't inspired by "easy." Seeing someone triumph over challenges with more perseverance than we judge ourselves to have inspires us to believe that we might be more capable than we currently believe. We get inspired to believe that perhaps we have a greater potential for strength and courage. We use our role models to lift the ceiling of our perceived limitations, therefore inspiring us to dream bigger, be braver, and feel more confident.

THERE IS A DIFFERENCE BETWEEN LIVING AND FEELING ALIVE

We don't learn anything from easy experiences. We also don't build confidence or challenge our endless capacity if everything is easy. If we calculate away too many opportunities because they are not easy enough to achieve, we are missing out on the most rewarding experiences that make us feel that we're not just living, but that we are alive.

Pay attention to what excuses come to mind when your dreams come calling. Remember you have a choice, and you are the only person who can limit your potential to reach your dreams. Remember that those we admire the most likely didn't get the metaphorical record deal on their first night. We relate to real people who aren't perfect. We are inspired by people who fought past the fear of their excuses, broke through limitations to which most others conceded, and who honored themselves to live their inspired life. We are inspired because we want to be that courageous.

Even the most successful people go through the same exact challenges in not letting excuses and rejection deter their dreams.

J.K. Rowling, multi-millionaire author of the Harry Potter series, had to overcome as a single mother on welfare.[10]

Theodor Seuss Geisel, better known as Dr. Seuss, received over 27 rejections from publishers before getting his break. In one rejection letter, Seuss was told that his work was "Too different from other juveniles on the market to warrant its selling."[10]

Vincent VanGogh sold only one painting in his lifetime and yet completed over 800 known works, not becoming famous until after his death.[10]

Soichiro Honda, founder of Honda Motor Company, was rejected by Toyota for an engineering job, unemployed for quite some time, expelled from college, survived severe illness, and even filed for bankruptcy before becoming successful.[10]

Walter Elias "Walt" Disney's first animation company went bankrupt and was rejected by more than 300 bankers before he was able to secure funding for his theme park. Early in his career, Walt Disney was fired by a newspaper editor because he "lacked imagination and had no good ideas."[10]

No matter what excuses or real limitations we may have, we can still get inspired. Whether we're facing physical, financial or circumstantial limitations, there are always opportunities to be inspired; many that don't require physical exertion, money or complete re-route of our lives.

ONLY YOU CAN ALLOW CEILINGS OF HAPPINESS

Those 10 ceilings of happiness are areas that inspiration may not be able to fix or transcend for you, meaning those struggles will always be a ceiling on your happiness until you resolve them. You must take care of yourself. You must advocate for yourself. Inspiration can take you higher than you've ever been before, but a ceiling is a ceiling. Free yourself to live a ceiling-less life. No one else can do that for you, and you deserve it.

"So many of us choose our path
out of fear disguised as practicality.

Fear is going to be a player in your life, but you get to decide how
much. You can spend your whole life imagining ghosts, worrying
about your pathway to the future, but all there will ever be is
what's happening here, and the decisions we make in this
moment, which are based in either love or fear."[1]

—Jim Carrey

CHAPTER EIGHTEEN

Make Room for Inspiration

You might have to clear out some old ways of thinking or acting to make room for inspiration. If you find yourself not having the life you want, it's time to make two more lists: complaints and excuses. List the complaints you have about your life. Go wild. Include big and little things, old and new, just let it flow—let it all out.

Next to your complaints, write excuses for why you can't or haven't done anything about these complaints. Don't hold back here, either. Is it someone else's fault? Are you waiting for something out of your control to occur? Will it take too long to see your desired result? Do you not know how? Do you not have enough time? Do you not have enough money? You might want to take a day of just adding to your list and exploring what comes up for you during that day. This list is only for you, so you might as well be as blatantly honest about how you truly feel.

On a different day, you can take inventory of what you wrote. Do any surprise you? Which charge you up the most? Now it's time to un-charge those excuses and complaints and determine what you can change or influence and what you can't.

If we can't change something, every moment we don't accept it and let it go from our grasp, we are unnecessarily choosing to sacrifice our happiness. We are creating distraction from living a happy life and causing ourselves mental and physical distress.

We might be more attached to the safety of our stories than we are to the true happiness unlocked by change. What would it take to let whatever *it* is go? Not for anyone else, but for yourself? C. JoyBell C. shares, "[Sometimes] you will find that it is necessary to let things go; simply for the reason that they are heavy."

I had to let go of some behaviors that were exhausting me simply because they were heavy. I didn't want to, I still had something to prove, but I chose to care about my happiness more than being right.

ARE YOU COMMITTED TO THE PROBLEM OR THE SOLUTION?

Every moment we spend internally (or vocally) complaining about something we can't or are unwilling to change or influence, we are choosing to be stuck in stress. We are telling the same story over and over so that we can stay committed to the problem, the victim role, or the comfortable feelings of everything being the same, even though we are complaining, stressed and vocalizing that we want things to be different.

Iyanla Vanzant states, "The only thing that goes on in your life is what you allow to go on in your life."

Having low self-worth is predictable. It's safe. It's dependable. Putting ourselves out there, we risk rejection. We are afraid to be vulnerable or risk "failure." Sadly it's easier to stay in old, negative patterns than to risk the vulnerability of change, rejection or uncertainty, but it is always our choice—a choice operated by fear.

Fear doesn't deserve our time or energy, and it certainly doesn't deserve sacrificing the fullness of our lives, happiness or health. Be honest, be accepting and be brave. We are no more or less entitled to living an inspired life than anyone else. It all comes down to the choice to pursue it.

If it's too hard to let all your worries, complaints and excuses go, try doing it a little at a time, but commit one step at a time to move forward on your path to letting go of old stories and making more room for inspiration.

BUT I DON'T HAVE TIME

If you find yourself seeking purpose, questioning the meaning of life, feeling victim to the daily grinds, or feeling helpless over doing too many things you "have" to do because you don't have time to do the things you "want" to do, take a moment to hit the refresh button on your perceived limitations, existing environment or stunted flow in life by making time for inspiration.

Time is our most precious resource. When we give our time to something or someone, it is a powerful statement of what is most important to us. I've learned to take ownership of my choices around "having time." We all have the same amount of hours in a day. Whether we choose to work for 12 hours or watch television for 12 hours, every minute is a choice and an undisputable decision on our priorities.

Time can be our greatest extension of love and care for others and ourselves. Just as we have to make time to text a friend when they're down or "show up" for an important event in our kid's life, we must "show up" for ourselves.

We have a plethora of ready excuses for why we can't afford the time to do self-care. They all might be real, but they are meaningless. We make time for what we want to make time for.

Work is a common reason people feel they don't have enough time. But even work is a choice. If work prevents you from creating time for self care, you could get a job with fewer hours. Maybe you love your job and don't want to change it, but you're still choosing not to make time for inspiration (unless your work is your inspiration).

Are you always running around with your kids, taking them from one activity to another? Find an hour a week while your child is attending an activity, or find a gym with day care, or ask a friend to babysit once a month to have some you-time to look forward to.

Find one hour a week for you—not to do laundry or clean the kitchen. If you are not making this time, you have to find a way. What are you choosing to do instead? It may be worth it, but it may not. We always have a choice, and sometimes the easiest option is not the most rewarding.

During my busiest time, I started listening to audiobooks in the car because that's when I "had time." I finally got to "read" all those books I had on my wish list and felt better about my commute. I started camping in the backyard on Saturday nights just to have a fun change of scenery throughout weekends that were otherwise consumed by building a business.

Just as choosing what to do matters, choosing what *not* to do has equal power. Choose not to spend so much time surfing the web. Learn a language during your commute. Balance time watching television (your break) with inspiring (recharging) activities. How can you be more present? What are you doing to avoid being present? Set parameters around when you check your email. Every choice is a choice of prioritization. Are you skipping breaks or working through every lunch? Can you take care of yourself a little more without getting fired?

There is always more to do at work, and we invite more work the more we stay after hours or work through lunches. We think we are just trying to keep up but we are setting the pace through setting expectations. Even in the busiest of times, you'll be happier and more productive if you find just five minutes to get inspired. Scents, songs, tastes...find something and enjoy the heck out of it for five minutes a day no matter what.

"You can't be brave if
you've only had wonderful things happen to you."

—Mary Tyler Moore

CHAPTER NINETEEN

Life is Hard; Inspiration is Easy

One of my favorite books, *The Road Less Traveled* by M. Scott Peck, M.D., begins with this thought: "Life is difficult." He continues, "Once we truly know that life is difficult—once we truly understand and accept it—then life is no longer difficult. Because once it is accepted, the fact that life is difficult no longer matters."[1]

Not only can life be hard, but being human can be hard. Being a kid can be hard. And being an adult can be hard.

If we reflect on the power we have to inspire ourselves, which can lead to unintentionally inspiring the world, we can approach acceptance that the struggles along our journey are precursors to our most inspiring moments. While inspiration is personal and originally experienced as a means to tap into and express who we truly are, our simple yet daring act of bravery to be ourselves and persevere becomes inspiring fuel for the world.

Until I began writing this book, I had a general sense that some of the hardships I've experienced in life helped me learn what I'm truly capable of, but I really still thought that the majority of the hardships were in vain.

I knew the epic and dramatic end of my last dysfunctional relationship turned my entire life upside-down, which prompted me to examine how it happened and find new tools to help me create a whole new, right-side-up life for myself.

I know now that I needed that experience to break patterns I didn't even realize were problems. That breakthrough helped me lift my ceiling of happiness in a way I never knew was possible.

But what about other facets of my life? The dysfunction and pain and anger that made me question my presence on this earth in childhood? That made life a relentless burden to endure when I was too young to make my own decisions, advocate for myself, or create the life I needed, wanted and deserved? I didn't know what to do with that until I began writing this book.

As an adult, I never needed to prove my hardships were any greater or lesser than anyone else's. Far too many humans experience hardships that create periods of soul-breaking pain, anger and sadness. Our soul can break in despair, but the pilot light of our spirit never goes out. It's just waiting for the fuel of inspiration to fire up and warm our bodies and slowly mend our soul.

As kids, we may not be able to obtain that fuel, but as adults, we can collect our inspired moments like kindling to feed that flame and regain our strength and sense of self. We can light our fire with sparks of inspiration until we feel warm and whole.

In diving in to discover how inspiration works, I realized that the role models I most admire, including those I admired as a child, all fought soul-breaking adversity.

How did Martin Luther King, Jr. or Rosa Parks have such a strong sense of self and conviction that their spirits could not be broken facing so much adversity? I am not that strong.

How did blind and deaf Helen Keller find and maintain the courage to fight for her life as she was being oppressed by the deathly judgment of World War II? I couldn't endure that kind of hardship with such an inspiring attitude.

How could *Soul Surfer*[2] Bethany Hamilton lose her arm and almost her life to a gruesome shark attack and get back in the water just one month later, refusing to let fear steal her inspiration? I am not that brave.

If you relate to my awe and humility toward the courage of these exceptionally inspiring role models, I'd like to humbly present a challenging question: Are we too quick to assume that any of us *couldn't* be strong, courageous or brave enough to endure these challenges?

We admire those who exhibit a spirit or courage or strength we *wish* we had, but *what if we do have those qualities,* but just haven't been tested in the same way? What if fear and circumstances are the only shadows standing between us and changing the world with the same strength, courage and bravery of those who inspire us?

I don't wish hardships on anyone, including myself. But I want to recognize that the hardships we have endured, and may yet endure, undoubtedly were or will be met with a strength, courage and bravery we may not know we possess until it is called into action.

If racism didn't exist, I doubt I would have known who Martin Luther King, Jr. was. If Helen Keller wasn't blind and deaf, her story likely wouldn't be read in schools and shared globally for so many decades. If Bethany Hamilton's arm hadn't been lost, a movie about her probably wouldn't have been made.

Because others have faced hardships, they have been able to remind us that we are capable of far more than we could imagine. We can't know how strong we are if we have never carried any weight.

When my happiness is threatened by experiences outside

my control, I process them as being wrong or unjust. I know in a textbook way that I learn and grow from each experience, but when I am in the throes of having my happiness threatened, I tend to not think about how important facing the challenge will be at a future time.

Now I can see those difficult times that threatened my spirit were not in vain. They were exercises to show and remind me that I am strong. They made me exceptional, unique, confident and ambitious. Challenges continue to remind me that I should never sell myself short of what I am capable.

Iyanla Vanzant shares, "Lives fall apart when they need to be rebuilt."[3] Challenges remind us who we are. Sometimes we are so disconnected from ourselves we need disruption to turn our world upside down because it's time for change. We may not think we are strong enough to initiate the change on our own, so we spiral until circumstances force us to re-route on a path back to our true selves. What feels like an anvil pulling us to the bottom is really the life preserver attached to our true selves, and we are being tugged back to the safety of the shore.

There are many devastating tragedies in which the "silver lining" viewpoint is too insensitive to apply, but when we endure and triumph over hardships, we are creating inspiring energy. We are a reminder to ourselves and others that we, as individuals and as a community, are stronger than we could have ever known until the moment we endured more than we previously thought possible. We are powerfully inspiring in every moment of fight and resiliency.

My stepmom Cindy, who broke her neck at 19 and has been using a wheelchair ever since, shocked me one day by saying, "I think breaking my neck saved my life. I was doing drugs and living a reckless life. Who knows where my life would have gone if I hadn't broken my neck."

Thinking about the moment she shared that still gives me pause. I can't imagine being able to attribute a big picture "benefit" to such a life altering experience. It has stuck with me that she had the courage to share this. It feels deeply personal, perhaps because I can't imagine being able to stop feeling sorry for myself long enough to be reflective about a silver lining if I was in similar circumstances.

But let's look at all that she was able to experience, much of which might not have happened if her accident didn't occur and she had continued on her destructive path of drug abuse.

She competed successfully in swimming on a national level, did whitewater rafting and pursued many other adventures. She gave birth to my sister and got to experience motherhood. She even quit smoking after 17 years when she was pregnant. Even through chronic pain, she holds a job as an elementary school librarian. She's an amazing cook and has a passion for creating lasting memories with our family. She has done a lot of personal work to overcome one of the worst childhoods I've heard of. Easy isn't a word I would use to describe any part of Cindy's life.

Her spirit in persevering when life isn't "easy" inspires me because I don't know if I could be that strong. She could have given up in many ways throughout her life. Through her example, I know if she can persevere, I can persevere. She is a great reminder to appreciate that I can walk, hike and run. She inspires me to not take physical freedom for granted and to keep a perspective when I think I'm having a "hard" time.

You may never know which specific moments of your life fuel someone's pilot light with inspiration when they need it most. Trust that you are inspiring and capable of providing hope to one or millions of lives just by being yourself along your life journey.

STEP 6:

Live the Inspired Life

"Don't tell me the sky's the limit
when there are footprints on the moon."

—Paul Brandt

CHAPTER TWENTY

Live the Inspired Life

We all have different journeys, but we share similar threads throughout the challenges and blessings of life. The threads of inspiration are the strongest.

Discovering what inspires someone is the easiest way to see the best in someone. Inspiration brings out our best, encouraging more loving or productive behavior and discouraging negative behavior. Inspiration may not solve one's deepest or darkest problems, but it can be a light when no other light shines. It can keep destructive behavior at bay.

Commonly, though quite personally, inspiration can save us. Music provides an opportunity for self-expression and is a companion that knows just how we feel. Sports can keep kids out of trouble and give them an opportunity to positively use physical energy, learning life skills through teamwork and good sportsmanship.

Inspiration builds self-esteem, it builds communities, and it builds lives. It creates paths where previous paths didn't exist. We don't have to have money to be inspired, but it can help us make money, and we're happiest when we work in a field related to what inspires us.

Connecting through inspiration helps those of us who feel alone feel less alone. The inspired life is living life in deepest connection with our true selves, acting on what we truly need, want and desire, and basing happiness on what is in our control. To know, love and honor our truest selves shapes our days, choices, feelings, fulfillment, success and happiness.

If I have learned anything along this journey of seeking inspiration and meeting inspiring people, it is that our judgment of others robs them from opportunities to be truly seen. Inspiration comes from within, but we have the power to put ceilings of happiness on other people. When you see someone with challenges you don't have, they don't want pity. They want to be seen in the same way we all do. Don't just act with kindness, *think* with kindness. Embrace our differences, instead of rejecting what we don't know or understand. Choose to see people.

We show our greatest strength when we choose to be vulnerable. Share your true self with strength and let others see you. Be curious about truth. As Dr. Anne Tomin once encouraged me, "be a truth seeker."

Intentionally look beyond surface barriers we put on others, no longer letting judgment block us from seeing another who is trying to share who they truly are.

Let moment after moment of inspiration compound to unveil a new way of experiencing life. Lean into inspiration and let go of the pursuit of happiness. We can live inspired and live connected to our passions, our interests and ourselves. We can choose activities that feed our souls, bodies, minds, curiosity and abilities. We can advocate for ourselves and share our true selves with the world.

It's your life. Don't let others' create it for you and don't want or expect anyone to change it for you. Circumstances are always mixed with opportunities and challenges. The best part is that you don't have to wait to live the inspired life. You can start right now, today.

Notes

Special Thanks To
1. Beattie, Melody. *Codependent No More*. Center City: Hazelden, 1986. Print.

Chapter Two
1. Harvard Business Review Staff. "The Science Behind the Smile." *Harvard Business Review*, January–February 2012. Web. 2 July 2015.

Chapter Four
2. Miller, Alice. *The Drama of the Gifted Child*. New York: Perennial, 1997. 103. Print.

Chapter Five
3. Louis Edlinger, Personal interview, 10 Aug. 2015.
4. Brigitte Thériault, Personal interview, 18 Aug. 2015.
5. Ronda Giangreco, Personal interview, 31 July. 2015.
6. Brown, Paul. "Basketball saved my life! Conner Washington is prime example why UK Sport should see sense." *Sunday Express*. Sunday Express, n.d. Web. 2 July 2015.
7. Wilczewski, William. "'Basketball saved my life,' says new RRHS coach." *Nogales International*. Nogales International, 26 Nov. 2013. Web. 2 July 2015.
8. Whitney, Xerxes. *What's Your Name*. Point Reyes: Xerxes Whitney, 1999. Print.
9. Whitney, Xerxes. *Busting Through: Exploring My Truth*. Healdsburg: Xerxes Whitney, 2007. Print.
10. Xerxes Whitney, Personal interview, 14 Aug. 2015.
11. Lorenzo Dughi, Personal interview, 17 Aug. 2015.

Chapter Ten

1. Thériault, Brigitte. *White Apron Chef*. White Apron Chef, 2005. Web. 15 Aug. 2015. <http://www.whiteapronchef.com/about>
2. Brandenburg, Josef. "Burn 450% More Fat in Half the Time With Interval Training." *Primer*. Primer Magazine, n.d. Web. 2 July 2015.
3. Blair, Beth. "How to Get 'in the Zone' for Faster Weight Loss." *Shape*. Meredith Women's Network, 14 May 2013. Web. 2 July 2015.
4. Black, Stephen. "Heart Rate Training for Weight Loss." *SpinFitness*. Mad Dogg Athletics, Jan 2009. Web. 2 July 2015.
5. Hay, Louise L. *You Can Heal Your Life*. Santa Monica: Hay House, 1987. Print.

Chapter Twelve
12. "work." *Merriam-Webster.com*. Merriam-Webster, 2015. Web. 2 July 2015.
13. Ferriss, Timothy. *The 4-hour Work Week*. Expanded and Updated ed. New York: Crown, 2009. Print.
14. Pam Chanter, Personal interview, 5 August 2015.
15. Jessica, Personal interview, 30 July 2015.

Chapter Seventeen
1. Jeffers, Susan J. *Feel the Fear and Do It Anyway*. San Diego: Harcourt Brace Jovanovich, 1987. Print.
2. Ruiz, Miguel. *The Four Agreements*. San Rafael: Amber-Allen, 1997. Print.
3. "selfish." *Merriam-Webster.com*. Merriam-Webster, 2015.Web. 2 July 2015.
4. "selfless." *Merriam-Webster.com*. Merriam-Webster, 2015.Web. 2 July 2015.
5. Vanzant, Iyanla (IyanlaVanzant). "You will never miss out on what is meant for you, even if it has to come to you in a roundabout way." 7 July 2015. 11:00 a.m. Tweet.

6. Rivera, Ryan. "Anxiety and the Brain: An Introduction." *Calm Clinic*. Calm Clinic, n.d. Web. 2 July 2015.
7. Hyman, Ira. "Don't Think About It." Web blog post. *Mental Mishaps*. Psychology Today, 10 Sept. 2010. Web. 2 July 2015.
8. Benjamin, Kathy and Dieter Melsens. "5 Ways Your Brain Is Tricking You Into Being Miserable." *Cracked*. Demand Media, 15 Apr. 2013. Web. 2 July 2015.
9. "The One Where Phoebe Hates PBS." *Friends*. National Broadcasting Company. KNTV, Santa Rosa. 18 Oct. 1998. Television.
10. Spencer, Jason. "Celebrities Who Overcame Adversity - Open Notes." Celebrities Who Overcame Adversity. Jason Spencer, 4 Feb. 2014. Web. 2 July 2015.

Chapter Eighteen

1. Carrey, Jim. Commencement Address. Maharishi University of Management. Golden Dome, Fairfield. 24 May 2014.

Chapter Nineteen

1. Peck, M. Scott. *The Road Less Traveled: A New Psychology of Love, Traditional Values, and Spiritual Growth.* New York: Simon and Schuster, 1978. Print.
2. *Soul Surfer*. Dir. Sean McNamara. Perf. AnnaSophia Robb, Dennis Quaid, Helen Hunt. TriStar Pictures, 2011. Film.
3. Vanzant, Iyanla. *Peace From Broken Pieces*. 5th ed. Carlsbad: SmileyBooks, 2012. Print.

ABOUT THE AUTHOR

Elaina Noell is an author, speaker, employee engagement consultant and certified Neuro-Linguistic Programming coach.

She traveled fearlessly into self-discovery when she desired greater happiness. After shedding layers of unhelpful patterns and assumed norms, she tapped into her true self, broke through the Ten Ceilings of Happiness, and started focusing on the transformative power of inspiration.

Believing that others could benefit from her journey, she felt compelled to offer practical and actionable dissections of the most common barriers to happiness and how to use inspiration to overcome them.

Realizing that the concept of focusing on inspiration instead of happiness was unspoken, she provides this new perspective on how real people can experience real happiness in an approachable and relatable way.

After completing this book, she quit her day job and backpacked South America for three months.

She is now the founder and principal of Inspiring Accountability in the Workplace, offering a fresh, practical and powerful approach to inspiring employee engagement, accountability and results. Her book, *Inspiring Accountability in the Workplace*, is available on Amazon.

Elaina also offers NLP Coaching sessions, trained by the best in the industry and offering "the most profound change work" she's experienced in terms of revising the moment limited beliefs were created in the subconscious.

Elaina knows through her personal experience as a client of NLP work that "everything is revisable, and everything is possible."

CONTACT

Web: www.elainanoell.com

Speaking: elaina@elainanoell.com

Facebook & Instagram: @ElainaNoell

ALSO AT

Web: www.inspiringaccountability.com

Instagram: @inspiringaccountabilityatwork